MASTERS OF THE FUTURES

Top Players Reveal the Inside Story of the World's Futures Markets

Scott Slutsky

Foreword by Leo Melamed

McGraw-Hill

New York   San Francisco   Washington, D.C.   Auckland   Bogotá
Caracas   Lisbon   London   Madrid   Mexico City   Milan
Montreal   New Delhi   San Juan   Singapore
Sydney   Tokyo   Toronto

Library of Congress Cataloging-in-Publication Data

Slutsky, Scott.
    Masters of the Futures : top players reveal the inside story of the world's
futures markets / [compiled by] Scott Slutsky ; edited by Darrell R.
Jobman.
      p. cm.
    Includes index.
    ISBN 0-07-134111-0
    1. Futures market. 2. Stockbrokers—Interviews. 3. Capitalists and
financiers—Interviews. I. Slutsky, Scott. II. Jobman, Darrell R.
HG6024.A3M377   1999
332.64'5—dc21   98-46144
                                                   CIP

McGraw-Hill

A Division of The **McGraw·Hill** Companies

1 2 3 4 5 6 7 8 9 0 DOC/DOC 9 0 3 2 1 0 9 8

ISBN 0-07-134111-0

The sponsoring editor for this book was Stephen Isaacs, the editing supervisor
was Donna Muscatello, and the production supervisor was Suzanne W. B.
Rapcavage. It was set in Fairfield by Carol Barnstable of Carol Graphics.

Printed and bound by R. R. Donnelley & Sons Company.

This publication is designed to provide accurate and authoritative information
in regard to the subject matter covered. It is sold with the understanding that
the author nor the publisher is engaged in rendering legal, accounting, fu-
tures/securities trading, or other professional service. If legal advice or other
expert assistance is required, the services of a competent professional person
should be sought.

> —*From a Declaration of Principles jointly adopted by a Committee of the
> American Bar Association and a Committee of Publishers.*

McGraw-Hill books are available at special quantity discounts to use as premi-
ums and sales promotions, or for use in corporate training programs. For more
information, please write to the Director of Special Sales, McGraw-Hill, 11
West 19th Street, New York, NY 10011. Or contact your local bookstore.

 This book is printed on recycled, acid-free paper containing a
minimum of 50% recycled de-inked fiber.

This book is dedicated to my sister and former business partner, Vicki, who is a master herself in coping with a challenge that is far greater than anything facing most open-outcry floor traders.

CONTENTS

FOREWORD

When reflecting on the dramatic changes that have transpired in global markets over the last two decades, one overriding truth must be considered: In our global market environment—an environment driven by instantaneous information flows and sophisticated technology—financial risk is ubiquitous and unending. Its management will continue to be the fundamental goal of investors and money managers.

The only question that is in contention is whether the present array of futures exchanges—where, to the greatest extent, the first genre of risk management tools were devised—can meet the critical challenges that have resulted from modern business sector transformations.

As nothing before, modern technology and over-the-counter products have created intense competitive considerations for the traditional futures exchanges. The issues are difficult and complex and have reached near-critical proportions. The answers by the exchanges will, at a minimum, determine whether futures markets will continue to play a meaningful role in risk management. In the meantime, the very existence of futures markets in the twenty-first century may be at stake. Scott Slutsky's *Masters of the Futures* offers a forum for thoughts from some of the top futures industry participants with respect to some of these issues. As such, publication of this book represents an important resource in the quest for the right solutions.

In reading this book and analyzing the responses of contributors, it is instructive for readers to remember that, until only a couple of decades ago, we had grown up secure in the knowledge that futures markets were the exclusive domain of agriculture. It was so from the time a young man named Joseph was separated from his 11 brothers and interpreted a dream for the

Pharaoh, a dream about seven lean years that were coming to the land of Egypt. Joseph's plan to put on forward buy-hedges in grains not only saved the Egyptian people from famine but also initiated the concept that futures markets would be limited only to agriculture.

It was so until the introduction of financial futures at the International Monetary Market of the Chicago Mercantile Exchange on May 16, 1972. This innovation created the first broad-based risk management instrument in foreign currency and ushered in the era of financial futures. Thereafter, expansion by futures exchanges into interest rate and index products—coupled with evolutionary forces in finance, global markets, and advancements of computer technology—transformed these relatively simple tools into the present genre of complex derivatives. Because this transformation has been so dramatic and swift and because financial derivatives have become so critical to the success of the American financial service sector, it is sometimes difficult to remember that the modern concept of financial derivatives as risk management tools is only two and a half decades old.

In a very real sense, the evolution of financial futures followed the general trend of the twentieth century, which moved the world from the vast to the infinitesimal. It is a trend that will surely continue. In physics, this century began with the theory of general relativity, which dealt with the big, with the universe. From there we journeyed to comprehension of the little, of quantum physics. Similarly, in biology we also moved from macro to micro—from individual cells to gene engineering. And in the financial markets, the process was strikingly parallel. When financial engineers applied advances in computer technology to established investment strategies, market applications went from the big to the little, just as in the sciences.

Charles Sanford, the former chairman of Banker's Trust, dubbed it "particle finance." The idea was to take every form of finance and investment—from alimony to zero coupon bonds—and break them up into tiny bundles of risk for trade.

One might even say that the Scottish-cloned sheep Dolly is the biological equivalent to its interest rate cousin, the interest rate swap.

Today, one cannot be in business without managing risk—that is to say, the application of derivatives. Indeed, the chairman of the U.S. Federal Reserve Board, Alan Greenspan, said as much in congressional testimony:

> The array of derivative products that has been developed in recent years has enhanced economic efficiency. The economic function of these contracts is to allow risks that formerly had been combined to be unbundled and transferred to those most willing to assume and manage each risk component.[1]

In other words, we live in a world where financial derivatives are used to protect against interest rate and exchange rate exposure, to manage assets and liabilities, to enhance equity and fixed-income portfolio performance and to protect against commodity price rises or mortgage interest expenses. As a consequence of their application, risks are reduced and profit is increased over a wide range of financial enterprises and in various ways—from businesses whose efficiency is enhanced to banks whose depositors and borrowers are benefited, from investment managers who increase their performance for clients to farmers who protect the value of their crops, from commercial users of energy to retail users of mortgages.

Clearly, the continued use of derivatives as tools in risk management in the next century is quite certain. However, the revolution launched in Chicago and copied in every corner of the globe now faces its most formidable challenge. The over-the-counter derivatives market greatly overshadows exchange-traded futures and options, and modern technology represents a grave challenge to the traditional transaction process of open

---

1 Testimony before the Subcommittee on Telecommunications and Finance of the Committee on Energy and Commerce, U.S. House of Representatives, May 25, 1994.

outcry. How will the exchanges respond to these challenges? Some of the answers are surely in this book.

Leo Melamed
CHAIRMAN EMERITUS
CHICAGO MERCANTILE EXCHANGE
NOVEMBER 1998

PREFACE

As I started to write this book, I thought, "Who will this book benefit? What can I write that will benefit anyone?"

If you have ever had a dream, if you have ever been told that you can't do it, if you have ever been told that you can't make it, this book is intended to encourage you to go for your dream or goal even though the world around you is changing. My floor trading world appeared to be on the verge of major changes. I wanted to know what the leaders of my profession thought about all these changes so I could chart my course for the future. The best course of action seemed to be just to ask them. That's how this book started.

Many people are depressed about the outlook for traditional open-outcry markets and futures trading, but the top futures industry players I interviewed for this book provided plenty of reasons to be optimistic about the future of futures. Yes, significant changes do lie ahead, but these leaders help you better understand what is likely to happen and what it will take for any trader to survive in this new trading environment.

Futures trading takes work. It is an accumulation of facts, style and guts. As a trader, you have basic rules that are simple to recite, hard to learn, and even more difficult to master. But that is no different from learning the rules and tactics of any intellectual game. The result of not following the rules is losses, and they hurt.

Like the fact that trading rules exist, it's a fact that changes in the futures industry will take place. What you will garner from the opinions and observations in the interviews in this book will not get you into a trading position at the low and out at the high, but it will broaden your understanding of what the futures industry is all about. The insights you get on the crucial issues facing the industry will provide you with the background you need to prepare for the changes as they unfold. If nothing else, this book should help you understand the global nature of finance and the dominant role technology will play in shaping our trading business in the years ahead.

Scott Slutsky
CHICAGO, ILLINOIS
NOVEMBER 1998

THE THIRD WAVE

By Darrell R. Jobman
Former Editor-in-Chief
Futures Magazine

The history of futures trading dates back a few hundred years to the ancient rice merchants in Japan or to the trade fairs of medieval Europe, depending on your source. Exactly what the futures "business" was like then probably will never be known. What is clear is that the concept of a centralized marketplace with standardized futures contracts traces its roots in the United States to the founding of the Chicago Board of Trade (CBOT) in 1848.

As that exchange and the futures industry looks back in observing a one-hundred fiftieth anniversary and looks ahead to a new century, it is also clear that traditional futures trading is in the midst of one of those periods of tremendous change when trading—and, indeed, business itself—is altered dramatically. What is happening today will have a profound effect on the way trading is done for years to come.

As futures trading evolved over the years, it produced its share of "names"— the R. N. Elliotts, W. D. Ganns, Jesse Livermores, Joe Leiters, and many, many others—some of them innovative pioneers, some of them trading legends, and some perhaps best described as just "characters." In more recent times, people such as Richard Donchian and Edward Gotthelf in the 1950s and 1960s began to bring more systemized approaches to trading that would be enhanced later by computers.

But, for the most part, the futures industry in which they operated remained pretty much the same for many years. The "modern" era of the futures industry started about 30 years ago when events began to come together that probably alarmed the old butter and egg traders at the Chicago Mercantile Exchange (CME) as much as some of today's developments are disturbing floor traders in the pits of the traditional open-outcry exchanges.

We are suggesting that what is happening in the futures and options industry today is a third major wave in the modern era—waves that altered or shaped the industry. Although the process of development is ongoing and cannot be defined by one or two events, the previous waves were sparked by a combination of factors that occurred within a relatively short period of time, producing a significant advance or a scary change, depending on your perspective. Each period included unprecedented fundamental events, totally new markets, totally new concepts for trading them, and a regulatory component as well—in other words, a time of paradigm shifts.

WAVE 1—MID-1970s

As you recount the events that occurred during this period, any one of them could have been market-stirring factors by themselves. Put them together and you have one of the most tumultuous eras in trading history.

Among the major fundamental factors were a series of events that took the prices of most physical commodities to levels never seen before—and, in a number of cases, not seen since. This was probably the first time most traders had ever heard of El Niño, the Soviet Union bought massive amounts of U.S. grain for the first time in 1972, the United States placed an embargo on soybean and meal exports, and in early September 1974, one of the earliest midwest frosts in history decimated soybean production—in short, weather and the resulting demand factors alone were enough to give the futures industry a whole new dimension on pricing in the 1970s.

Then add a mideast oil embargo that brought lines at U.S. gas stations and an escalation in energy prices, wage and price controls that only made matters worse, the end of a military and political disgrace in Vietnam, a U.S. president involved in scandal and eventually resigning on August 9, 1974, a steep economic recession and sharp setback in the U.S. stock market . . .. There were certainly enough fundamental factors present to affect the course of futures trading.

But, as far as the futures industry itself is concerned, perhaps the single biggest development of that period was the realization that the biggest commodity of all is money. Led by Leo Melamed and the so-called "young Turks," the CME opened the door to financial futures when it launched trading in currency futures on May 16, 1972. The next step for financial futures was the first interest rate futures contract on GNMAs, which the Chicago Board of Trade (CBOT) began trading on October 20, 1975.

The CBOT was also involved in another major development during that period, spinning off the Chicago Board Options Exchange as a new exchange to trade a few equity call options on April 26, 1973. After starting slowly, this was the beginning of what was to become a hugely successful new instrument that would have a wide appeal to traders.

All these developments might not have occurred except for an updated regulatory environment. After a series of "London commodity options" scandals and with the new financial and gold contracts to oversee, Congress decided to set up a separate agency to regulate futures. The Commodity Futures Trading Commission (CFTC) was activated on April 21, 1975, and, after the typical early organizational struggles, approved trading in T-bills and T-bonds a few years later. The move into financials greatly expanded the horizon for futures. The Securities and Exchange Commission (SEC), after a long battle, provided the approval that launched the equity options segment of the investment spectrum.

WAVE 2—EARLY 1980s

Like Wave 1, there were plenty of fundamental factors at work in the early 1980s. Included in that background were another grain embargo—this time inspired by politics and not supply—weather and government program impacts on crop production, another Organization of Petroleum Exporting Countries oil embargo, rampant U.S. inflation, unprecedented prices for gold and silver, soaring interest rates, a major shift in U.S. Federal Reserve policy—again, all by themselves, any one of these factors could account for significant shifts in trader thinking.

In this period, it was the shift in the regulatory structure that was probably the key to perhaps the largest number of the most substantial changes in the shortest amount of time in the history of the futures industry. After a lengthy stalemate over almost every issue at a time when the CFTC's primary function was to throw sand in the gears of progress, as some futures industry leaders viewed it, the change in presidential parties in the 1980 election led to the appointment of Philip McBride Johnson as the new CFTC chairman.

It was like a breath of fresh air bringing new vitality to the futures industry. Under Johnson's leadership, the CFTC approved totally new concepts that opened the door to many of today's most successful contracts.

The first was the launch of the CME Eurodollar futures contract on December 9, 1981, the first cash-settled contract that did not require delivery of the underlying instrument. Without cash settlement, a number of today's contracts would not exist.

The second was approval for stock index futures, cash-settled contracts that required the negotiation of the Johnson-Shad Agreement at the top levels of the CFTC and SEC to determine who had jurisdiction over which markets. The Kansas City Board of Trade started trading the first stock index futures contract on the Value Line Index on February 24, 1982, and other stock indexes soon followed, although it took more than 15 years to bring Dow Jones Industrial Average contracts to the exchange floors.

The third major industry-shaping approval by the CFTC under Johnson was for options on futures contracts. After nearly 10 years of trying to develop an options program, the CFTC approved a pilot program that allowed each exchange to trade options on just one futures contract beginning October 1, 1982. As these contracts proved themselves, exchanges slowly received permission to expand trading in options on futures.

Another major new physical commodity market also came into its own during this period as the New York Mercantile Exchange added gasoline and then crude oil futures to a revised heating oil futures contract that it had been trading for a few years. Although virtually every other widely used physical commodity was covered by a futures contract, this was new territory, and energy futures soon became one of the most actively traded commodity areas.

These new U.S. developments during the early 1980s triggered the development and launch of new exchanges and new contracts around the globe in the following years, especially in the financial areas. The repercussions from Wave 2 continue to be felt in the world marketplace as trading has turned into a global 24-hour affair that has had a major impact on exchange alignments and many other facets of how trading can be done today.

WAVE 3—LATE 1990s

Just as the ripples forward from Waves 1 and 2 continue to affect trading today, the ripples that are producing Wave 3 go back a number of years. In fact, it probably is more difficult to put any specific time frames on Wave 3, but the conclusion is the same: The futures industry is in the midst of a major change, not so much in what market or instrument is traded this time but in how they are traded. The industry has developed remarkably in the years since the early 1980s, particularly in its international scope and growth, but events that started to come together more clearly in 1998 appear to be producing another significant wave of change.

Just as in the earlier waves, there are fundamental factors that are so significant that they can change traders' long-held perceptions of a market. On this list might be the unprecedented climb in many stock markets beyond anyone's imagination a few years ago, a decline in prices for some physical commodities to levels not seen in many years—in some cases, to pre-1970s explosion levels that many did not expect to see again—severe economic problems in areas such as the Far East,

Russia, and Latin America, the move into the European Economic and Monetary Union and a new currency unit, the coming millenium when who knows what Year 2000 computer glitches could disrupt many aspects of our daily lives—in short, any of these fundamental factors alone is enough to have a major bearing on market outlook.

But, as with the earlier waves when you can point to one or two developments that sparked significant change, the key to change in futures trading in the late 1990s is technology. Although mainframe computers helped the futures industry grow during the earlier waves, the personal computer was not even available to an earlier generation of traders. Now it is everywhere and has become a widespread tool. With the development of the Internet, intranets, online brokerage services, instantaneous news and quotes, and many other features, the personal computer is changing the way people approach trading. If there are markets for Beanie Babies® or automobiles or just about anything else on the Internet, attempts at other markets, including futures, probably are not far behind.

No one gave much credence to an early attempt to set up electronic trading, the International Futures Exchange Inc. (Bermuda), or INTEX, which was launched on October 25, 1984, but could never drum up much support or build enough volume to survive. U.S. futures exchanges seemed to dismiss any idea of an electronic trading alternative until the CME unveiled plans for what would become Globex. First announced in 1987 a month before the Black Monday stock market crash, Globex did not make its first trade until 1992. Meanwhile, exchanges outside the United States and the equity options exchanges picked up on the electronic trading concept and ran with it. Then in 1998 momentum in that direction began to pick up in a big way. This was an idea whose time had come.

Now everyone in the world seems to be shifting to or talking about electronic trading systems. As various electronic systems develop, they will have an impact far beyond the trading floors. The processing of orders and execution of trades will change for virtually everyone, and it looks like we are in the middle of another wave that calls for a paradigm shift in trading.

So how will this wave unfold? How will trading be done in the next 5 to 10 years? Will the traditional open-outcry methods survive? How will exchanges respond to changes? How will brokerage firms help their customers? How will the regulators react?

Those questions are the premise of this book. Probably no one can accurately predict the answers, but the people who are likely to come closest are the leaders who not only reflect years of experience and perspective from the past but also are in the key positions that will shape the industry in the future. These are the "masters of the futures," who will have a major influence on the way you will trade as we go into the next century.

ACKNOWLEDGMENTS

I would like to thank all of those people who helped me learn this exciting futures trading business and all the masters of the futures industry who participated in this project. I especially want to thank a few special people:

My wife, Julie, for listening to my dreams and ideas and understanding that a telephone call at 2:30 a.m. was not intended to wake up the family but was dialed during someone's normal work day in another part of the world.

My children, Sean, Danny, Eric and Adam, who make me smile and make everything worthwhile.

My parents, Lee and Nate Slutsky, for getting me into the futures business and for loving and nurturing me throughout my life.

Norma Newberger, for believing in me all these years and providing support in everything I undertake.

Jack Sandner, for his guidance and encouragement throughout this project.

Marrietta, Terina and LeeAnn, the office staff, for putting up with me and all my requests.

The staff members of many of the participants, for relaying messages and information back and forth and enduring my persistent inquiries.

MASTERS OF THE FUTURES

THE COMPETITIVE EDGE

Patrick H. Arbor
Chairman
Chicago Board of Trade

Patrick H. Arbor is serving his third two-year term as chairman of the Chicago Board of Trade (CBOT) and also is chairman of the MidAmerica Commodity Exchange. He previously served several terms on the CBOT board of directors, including a term as vice chairman from 1987 to 1989, after first being elected to the board in 1980, and he has served on many exchange and futures industry committees.

An independent futures trader, Arbor also is a principal in the trading firm of Shatkin, Arbor, Karlov & Co. He started his career as a math teacher before becoming a member of the CBOT in 1965.

Active in government and community affairs, charitable organizations, and banking, Arbor was appointed in October 1994 by President Clinton to the board of directors of the Western New Independent States Enterprise Fund, charged with promoting private sector development in Belarus, Moldova, and Ukraine. He also serves as a member of the advisory board for the U.S. Association for the United Nations High Commissioner for Refugees, sits on the executive committee of the

Board of Trustees of Loyola University, and is a member of the board of regents of Chicago's Mercy Home for Boys and Girls.

Arbor is a veteran mountain climber who has scaled many of the world's tallest peaks.

The CBOT observed its one-hundred-fiftieth anniversary in 1998 and has long been the world's largest and most active futures exchange. As chairman of this leading exchange, you have had a key role in many significant futures industry developments in recent years. As you look ahead, what do you see as the single most important futures industry issue or development in the next few years?

Arbor: Several developing trends are presently shaping the destiny of the futures industry:

- Consolidations and mergers
- Cross-pollination of markets
- Impact of electronic trading platforms

Singling out any one trend is difficult because all of these developments are interrelated. Nevertheless, electronic trading clearly is effecting a paradigm shift, the ramifications of which promise to radically restructure the industry pioneered by the CBOT 150 years ago.

As a trading methodology, open outcry has serviced the futures industry well, and there is no reason to believe it cannot continue to be a valuable system for facilitating price discovery and risk management. Open-outcry auction markets create the critical mass, the liquidity, and the efficiency to support the basic economic function of futures.

However, the development of viable, dynamic electronic trading systems, if not indeed creating a new order, is calling for a reassessment of how this business is conducted. In tandem with new technological underpinnings to enhance the efficacy of floor trade, computerized trading systems should create new opportunities for market participants and, indeed, open the marketplace to a greater number of participants.

We have barely begun to explore the potential of the Internet firmament, which promises to become a critical tool in the further development of derivatives markets. Although I remain an advocate for the effectiveness of open-outcry markets, the CBOT nonetheless will be prepared to utilize all manner of technology that will service the needs of our members and customers.

What is the outlook for open outcry over the longer term?

Arbor: Despite the trend toward computerized trading, despite even the CBOT's movement toward listing financial products on Project A concurrently with our pit trade, I remain bullish on open outcry. CBOT volume during the first half of 1998 was up more than 18 percent from the record pace a year earlier, and there is every reason to believe this growth will continue.

Open outcry brings together critical mass, transparency, liquidity, and excellent execution. Glitches in the system are few because the human trading engine never fails as can happen with computerized systems. That being said, I remain a believer in market darwinism and realize that natural selection will dictate that the strongest form of trading will survive. Accordingly, the CBOT is embracing both methodologies and will let the market determine which will dominate trading in the future.

Having said that, I should mention that, in Chicago, we grow traders like the Swiss grow bankers and the Italians grow designers. These traders, born into the open-outcry auction market, are unique among the world's trading population. They are unparalleled risk-takers and will not go gently into the good night of electronic trading. Consequently, I expect we will see a new market hybrid, one in which electronic trade will coexist with open outcry. Further, I expect agricultural markets to continue to flourish in an open-outcry forum.

In addition to electronic trading, how will other technological developments affect traders and the exchange?

Arbor: Internet-integrated technology looms like a new star in the firmament, promising to shed tremendous light on traditional systems. In addition to computerized trading applications, I believe we will witness related applications in order routing. These will serve to complement, and possibly replace, certain systems now in use or in development, such as wireless order transmission over headsets. There is too much on the horizon—from such Internet applications to possible implementation of virtual reality systems—that even Nostradamus might have a difficult time effectively answering questions on technology.

How important is the electronic order routing you mentioned?

Arbor: Electronic order routing is the key to longevity for open-outcry exchanges and their traders. By routing orders directly to and from the pit, automated routing will make trading faster, less expensive, and overall, more efficient. The CBOT is serious about moving to a paperless trading environment because it represents a critical path toward cost reduction and increased efficiency.

You have already taken significant steps in the electronic direction with Project A, which has been expanded to daytime hours. How could traders use Project A even more effectively?

Arbor: First, traders must continue to learn the Project A system. Due to the tremendous growth of Project A, the CBOT registration lists remain quite lengthy. Beyond that, the older generation of traders must realize the importance of carrying the arrow called Project A in their quivers. The younger generation is computer literate and tends to gravitate naturally to the opportunities offered by Project A. Established market participants can ill afford to overlook these opportunities.

Without question, Project A represents a challenge to further understand the integration of the CBOT's trade with the globalized trade of foreign financial instruments ranging from German bunds to the various Euro products. When I came to the CBOT, I was fortunate enough to learn about the interrelationship of different commodities and different commodity months. As a result, I became a spreader and was able to capitalize on different opportunities. After-hours trade on Project A offers similar, although new, opportunities such as T-bond/Euro arbitrage at 3 in the morning and just might hold some interesting possibilities.

With the new Euro and other new trading possibilities, what contracts or markets are most vulnerable to change in the next 5 to 10 years?

Arbor: All contracts are vulnerable to change, and that's why the CBOT continuously reviews contract specifications to ensure they are appropriate for the market. Our effort to overhaul delivery terms of the corn and soybean contracts is an example of how we change our contracts to reflect market activity.

Obviously, no one can positively assess the impact of the Euro on global currency trade. Although certain opportunities in foreign exchange will simply disappear, I see tremendous new opportunities opening up, especially during the first two years following the introduction of the Euro, when national currencies will still be in circulation.

The increasing sophistication of market participants could threaten the established contract markets. Forward rate agreements, for example, could pose a strong challenge to the dominance the Eurodollar contract has held on the short end of yield curve trade. Any synthetic new trade could threaten the contracts so widely used today, just as the over-the-counter markets have cannibalized the exchange-traded market share.

**One of the newer contract areas at the CBOT is the Dow
Jones Industrial Average. What are your projections for
trading the Dow?**

Arbor: There is nothing but upside for the CBOT Dow contracts. Despite admirable competing products, as well as problems with some 500,000 Series 7 license holders not being able
to offer their customers our Commodity Futures Trading Commission (CFTC)-regulated product, we have seen greater
growth in our Dow complex than any other contract group in
our history. Berries don't ripen overnight, nor will the CBOT's
Dow products mature faster than they should. Maturity takes
time, but clearly, we are witnessing measurable hallmarks of
growth and success.

**Why trade the Dow at the CBOT rather than one of the
other exchanges that offer Dow products?**

Arbor: Because we offer a good-sized contract that provides an
ideal hedging vehicle for the actual Dow index. And we've got
risk-takers in both the futures and options who are there to
make it happen.

**One area of concern for some traders is the impact
funds sometimes have on prices. How can the retail
trader cope with the clout of the funds?**

Arbor: That's easy: Sell high, buy low. Seriously, the impact of
the funds is tremendous and should keep the timid or undercap-
italized from such trading. However, in both open-outcry pit
trading and electronic pit trading—that is, exchange-based electronic trade—there is an egalitarianism of trade. Like the elec-
tive affinities of a chemical reaction, magnum offers, magnum
bids. In the case of the T-bond pit at the CBOT, for example,
this trade gravitates to the top step of the pit, whereas activity of

a smaller size is executed elsewhere within the pit. There's room for everybody to play.

Would traders benefit from a two-tier system?

Arbor: Absolutely not. The CBOT is now fighting hard against noncompetitive trading—block trading—because it would drain liquidity from the pits and result in an unlevel playing field for all but a relatively few market participants. Exchange trading has always championed equal-opportunity trading. I do not see that changing.

How about common clearing, another issue in the news? How beneficial would that be for the futures industry, brokerage firms, traders?

Arbor: Common clearing must be viewed in the proper perspective of market evolution. As the CBOT moves toward a common clearing platform with the Chicago Mercantile Exchange, we must be aware that this represents but one small, though critical, step in this evolution. Neither exchanges nor market participants can afford to tap dance on the conventions of the past. We must move forward, evaluating all systems in light of an order that is changing rapidly.

The importance of reducing the cost of conducting business is a given. It remains the domain of exchange leadership to determine the most effective steps to reach this goal. Common clearing will decrease costs and increase efficiency by combining systems and eliminating duplicative, unnecessary functions. Again, however, it represents but one measure that needs to be implemented. We must think outside the box, outside the region, looking beyond parochial walls and traditional borders to recognize transformational business opportunities, as well as the means of realizing these opportunities in the most efficient and cost-effective manner.

Fifteen years ago, over-the-counter commodity transactions were only a concept. Today, they are a vibrant reality. Demarcations have blurred as we have come to realize that traditional borders are only a connection to another side, another reality. Although common clearing still poses problems of logistics, implementation, and provincialism, we have every intention of implementing it for the improvement of our marketplace and of continuing to look beyond conventional restrictions to further embrace significant change that will create more effective exchanges and a stronger overall marketplace.

What about linkages with other international exchanges?

Arbor: International exchange linkages no longer represent the shock of the new. As time zones and national borders collapse in the black hole of the future, we are left with fewer strictures that can impede exchange and market growth. Linkages and mergers of all sorts have become de rigeur, no matter the industry, and the futures industry is no different.

As existing orders change and the Berlin walls of regionalism are torn down, we must look to all four corners for opportunities that will strengthen and deepen our markets. International linkages are the natural result of the 24-hour trading day and the globalization of the financial marketplace. The CBOT's linkage with Eurex personifies this as we merge the old and the new while infusing tradition with the spark of technology. This particular linkage personifies the CBOT's goal of creating new opportunities for its members and customers while expanding the reach of its core products by utilizing the very best of bleeding-edge technology.

A number of new concepts and proposals could have a significant impact on the futures and options industry. We can't cover all of them, because there seem to be new announcements every week, but we would like your

comments on a few developments. Let's start with the Cantor Fitzgerald proposal for the Cantor Exchange.

Arbor: Substantial legal deficiencies should have prevented the CFTC from moving forward on the application for the Cantor Exchange, as we outlined in letters to the CFTC. For the Commission to approve such a legally flawed application undermines the Commission's credibility with all market participants as an agency devoted to enforcing the law.

But now that the Cantor Exchange is trading, bring them on. Although we take any competitive threat seriously, especially when one floats on such thin air, the Cantor Exchange—or anyone else, for that matter—has a long way to go before it can touch the liquidity and execution of the CBOT's financial markets. Open outcry might seem like chaos to the uninitiated, but any satisfied futures commission merchant will tell you there is a grand elegance there.

In other industries we've seen newcomers giving away their products on the street, just to get people to try them. However, any product, no matter how inexpensive—no matter even if it's free—will not be accepted on a wide scale if a better one exists. The CBOT not only has the product, but we're getting better all the time.

Chicago Board Brokerage (CBB) formed by the CBOT and Prebon Yamane?

Arbor: CBB will provide the most advanced and customer-friendly trading system for cash treasuries in the world. Such a platform, alongside CBOT futures markets, creates myriad opportunities for all manners of trade, from basis trades to repos to an endless array of multilegged transactions. Players on CBB will benefit from cross-margining and triple A clearing as well.

In phase two, we will utilize the expertise of our CBB partner, Prebon Yamane, and list customized transactions that will bring the benefits of customization and flexibility—typically found in the over-the-counter markets—to our exchange marketplace.

DTB-SOFFEX (Deutsche Terminbörse and Swiss Options and Financial Futures Exchange) merger to form Eurex?

Arbor: Creating this pan-European exchange does two things: (1) It takes a giant step toward a unified, harmonized marketplace that will benefit all market participants, and (2) it reflects the universal trend toward mergers and consolidations. Bolstered by tensile-strength technology, Eurex becomes a natural partner for the CBOT. We anticipate that our alliance will be in place and operational by July 1999 and that it will capitalize on our respective strengths and our great products to remain in the forefront of world financial trade. I am very excited about this partnership and what it bodes for the CBOT.

DTB terminals in the United States?

Arbor: DTB already has terminals at member firms in the United States and has asked the CFTC to expand its network to U.S. customers. The CBOT believes the CFTC should approve this link because there are no deterrents to installing U.S. futures exchange terminals in Germany.

The rapid transition to electronic trading at Matif (Marché a Terme International de France)?

Arbor: Matif's migration to an electronic platform has been successful, and we laud them for that. It is a relatively young exchange with a different type of membership from that of the CBOT, so the transformation was relatively smooth, as was expected. However, as evidenced by the July 23, 1998, trading error that caused their bond price to crash, electronic trade contains hazards that are not present when the trading engine is a human one. All exchanges must learn from those types of unfortunate problems so that we do not forsake the great value of face-to-face trading in a mad rush to computers.

The decision by LIFFE (London International Financial Futures Exchange) to go public and its plans for electronic trading?

Arbor: Unlike LIFFE, the CBOT made a strategic decision long ago to build a new trading floor and pursue first-rate electronic trading for overnight markets. Our growing volume proves that the CBOT made the right decision on both counts.

When I became chairman of the CBOT, my first goal was to create the world's best trading facility. We needed it, and we needed it right away. Accordingly, it has facilitated tremendous growth and opportunity. LIFFE, regrettably, never made that decision.

As much as I emanate from the open-outcry milieu, it has been very clear that the CBOT must have a world-class trading system. Accordingly, we have increased the capacity of Project A and are working with our Eurex partners to further enhance our electronic capabilities. Regrettably, LIFFE never capitalized on what was a very good start with its APT system.

The CBOT made a commitment to its members' legacy and built the world's largest, most advanced trading hall. Further, we made a very conscious decision to be prepared for the electronic evolution of the marketplace. These two decisions create the foundation of a far-reaching strategic plan that should help us maintain our competitive edge well into the next century. We have kept an eye on our competitors and potential competitors and have remained a step ahead.

In addition to industry developments, what economic developments will affect markets in the next 5 to 10 years?

Arbor: Certain ones are easy to spot—the introduction of the Euro and instability in Asia. Generally speaking, it's the great trend toward consolidations, as seen in the case of the European Economic and Monetary Union (EMU) and the overall *pax orbis terrarum*. Although the world is not free from problems, we are not engaged in a conflict on the scale of the world wars or even the Vietnamese war. Such a tableau makes it a more difficult trade in the derivatives markets, which thrives on volatility. However, something usually comes along to shake things up. Certainly, the global currency markets and the Asian crisis hold the potential for a great tsunami that could wash over the shores of a low-volatility environment.

CHAPTER

T W O

THE NEW BOARD OF TRADE

James J. Bowe
President and Chief Executive Officer
Board of Trade of the City of New York

James J. Bowe was appointed president and chief executive officer of the Board of Trade of the City of New York in June 1998 following its creation as the parent company in the merger of the Coffee, Sugar & Cocoa Exchange, Inc. (CSCE) and the New York Cotton Exchange (NYCE). In this capacity, he also serves as president and CEO of both the CSCE and the NYCE.

Prior to becoming president of the CSCE in April 1996, Bowe was the senior vice president of market development and planning at the CSCE for 15 years, responsible for the research and development of new trading instruments and for the marketing, public relations, economics, market surveillance, and related planning functions of the exchange.

Bowe began his financial industry career in 1973 at the National Association of Securities Dealers. In 1977, he joined the Commodity Exchange Inc. (COMEX), where he served as vice president of marketing and new product development after having responsibilities for financial surveillance and audit functions. He moved to Fahy International Trading Corporation as vice president of financial futures in 1980 prior to assuming his position at the CSCE in 1981.

Bowe is active in many industry associations and is currently serving as a director of the National Futures Association. He has also served on the board of the Managed Futures Association.

In the midst of all the mergers and affiliations and all the other recent developments at exchanges worldwide, your exchange has been one of the major news makers. Going back more than 20 years to the time four New York futures exchanges got together to share one trading floor at the Commodity Exchange Center in the World Trade Center, there has always been the thought that the New York exchanges might merge into one exchange for some of the same reasons driving today's mergers—consolidating operations to make trading more efficient and cost-effective.

The number of New York futures exchanges has now been narrowed to two. Because it's a new and different structure for a merger, let's start with some background on the Coffee, Sugar & Cocoa Exchange getting together with the New York Cotton Exchange to form the Board of Trade of the City of New York.

Bowe: It's interesting that you go all the way back to the move into the World Trade Center (July 1977). That move preceded the merger of the New York Cocoa Exchange and the New York Coffee & Sugar Exchange in 1979. That was solely a cost-saving move—it had become just too expensive for the Cocoa Exchange to be housed in a separate facility, so it merged with Coffee & Sugar and came over to the World Trade Center, putting five New York futures exchanges on one floor. It was a true merger where the two exchanges became one, and all the seats enjoyed identical privileges.

The more recent merger between the New York Cotton Exchange and the Coffee, Sugar & Cocoa Exchange that closed on June 10, 1998, is being done in phases. Given the disparity between seat values, we decided to offer members payments as well as promissory notes to bring the two seat values to equality. What we basically had were two seats with a price difference of about $75,000, as well as significantly different exchange net worths.

The notes and payments that have been issued come to $100,000 for each member of Coffee, Sugar & Cocoa Exchange and $25,000 to each member of the Cotton Exchange. These amounts will be paid in seven installments, the first having been issued the week of the closing and the rest annually for six more years. When the notes are completely paid off, the two seats will become one, and each of the members of the individual exchanges will then have privileges to trade all the products on both exchanges.

The notes are guaranteed by a letter of credit, so the members are assured they will get their payments. It is our expectation that the savings from the merger will fund the payment of the notes over time. The members clearly believed they were participating in a fair deal, with more than 80 percent of the members who voted in each exchange casting ballots in favor of the merger.

How will this affect the divisions of the Cotton Exchange such as FINEX or the Citrus Associates?

Bowe: They continue to function as they did prior to the merger. Right now, for example, Citrus Associates is the Commodity Futures Trading Commission's (CFTC) designated contract market for the orange juice contract. The designated markets remained the same to streamline the process of completing the merger. By keeping the NYCE subsidiaries with their existing rules and processes, we didn't have to start writing a new rulebook and going through the whole designation process for the new exchange with the CFTC.

The merger arrangement sounds like a good one for the exchanges. What about the members of the exchanges? What does a cotton member, say, gain from this merger?

Bowe: In the short term, members gain the payment stream, and they gain efficiencies of having one administration for the markets, one set of financial statements, lower costs—costs will be reduced by about $7.5 million a year. At the end of six years, they gain the right to trade any of the products on the combined exchange.

In addition, part of the transaction involves ownership of the Cantor Exchange Inc. The Cantor Exchange has been set up as a limited liability corporation where the exchange will receive 10 percent of profits and the members will receive 90 percent of profits coming from exchange and clearing fees. The Cantor Exchange deal will result in a payment stream to the members of the New York Board of Trade (NYBOT) as well as positioning them on the leading edge of technological change in the United States.

The Cantor Exchange will utilize the existing screen system that Cantor uses for interest rate products, currency, and currency options dealings and lists futures products on the cash government securities trading screen. This means that the more than 20,000 screens worldwide that Cantor already has on traders' desks will have direct access to our new futures products. Because Cantor does approximately half of all the daily cash business in the government securities market, connecting a futures market into the same system spells success.

This operation will be screen-based, of course. Is the exchange's philosophy to go toward screen-based trading for everything, as seems to be occurring at exchanges in Europe and elsewhere, or to maintain open outcry along with the screens?

Bowe: We believe it makes sense to trade financial products on a screen because it can be more efficient. There is a dramatic difference, however, in the way financials trade and how agricultural (ag) products trade. The financial futures contracts derive their value from cash market prices whereas the ag markets really don't have liquid cash markets where they can obtain price discovery. In fact, price discovery for ag products occurs in the trading pit, and the cash price of a commodity such as sugar or cotton is quoted at a premium or discount to the futures price.

It doesn't sound like much, but it's a significant difference in how price discovery takes place. Look how bonds trade; they trade at a price. The price discovery happens in the cash market. The ag futures products might not lend themselves as efficiently to computerized trading. They may continue to need the pit to perform the price-discovery function.

So this is not a decision to go electronic totally some day?

Bowe: That is absolutely correct. But it does put us in a very enviable position in that we have access to a computerized platform if it eventually appears that the ag markets need to be traded in a computerized environment. We could add them to the Cantor network quickly.

What is your reaction to the Chicago Board of Trade (CBOT) "shot across the bow" announcement that it might try to trade its own coffee, sugar, and cocoa futures on its Project A system—sort of an if-you-do-that-we'll-do-this retaliatory move for your Cantor deal?

Bowe: Our initial reaction, frankly, was surprise that the CBOT would act in that manner. We suggested to them that if they think ag markets trade well on a computer, how about soybeans, corn, or wheat, which are much larger markets than what we have here in New York.

So you are suggesting that if trading in ag products indeed does work on screens, you could try trading soybeans or corn or wheat on your screens in New York?

Bowe: Well, it's not even that. If the CBOT were sincere in thinking computers should be used for trading ag products, wouldn't it seem logical that they would want to protect their own existing marketplaces rather than threaten us?

Let's go back to your setup with Cantor. How will that work for your current traders?

Bowe: Our existing members can have direct access to the Cantor System through the new exchange. Initially, the Cantor Exchange will be handled through terminal operators the way Cantor does cash business today, but in a few months everyone will be able to have a direct computer interface with the Cantor System. All transactions will still have to clear through an exchange clearing member. Individual members registered with the National Futures Association and representatives of members can receive authorization to trade through a fairly easy process. Those individuals will be coded through the system, so we will be able to track everything that's done. In fact, we will have the most complete audit trail that exists.

What have you learned from the experiences with electronic trading at DTB (Deutsche Terminbörse), Matif (Marché a Terme International de France), or elsewhere?

Bowe: What happened at the DTB in competing electronically with the London International Financial Futures Exchange (LIFFE) open-outcry system in the German bund has shown that financial products do work well in a computerized trading system. The fact that DTB was able to go so quickly from a 30 percent market share to a 90 percent share indicates the power of the computer for trading financial products and really validates the wisdom of the deal we have with Cantor.

What about other exchange mergers taking place—the American Stock Exchange with NASDAQ and Philadelphia Stock Exchange, the Chicago Board Options Exchange with the Pacific Stock Exchange, and others? How do you see the whole trading scenario shaping up?

Bowe: Basically, the exchanges are just like a lot of financial service businesses. There are efficiencies that can be achieved through merger that are beneficial to the members. To the extent those opportunities exist, the boards of the exchanges are obliged to look at them. If the deals are viable, we have to move forward.

I don't know if that means there will be more mergers over the next couple of years, but recent events show there are ways to achieve efficiencies and that computerized trading is going to be a competitive issue among the exchanges. The exchange that offers the most liquidity with the cheapest execution cost is going to be where the business gets done. To protect the interests of our members, we need to be on the cutting edge of that decision-making process.

What about the next step in New York, a merger with the New York Mercantile Exchange (NYMEX) to form one exchange there?

Bowe: Right now there are no active discussions between NYMEX and the New York Board of Trade. We did talk to NYMEX about getting space in its trading facility, but that facility was built for NYMEX and not the whole New York community. There simply wasn't adequate space there for us. To the extent the situation changes or if we introduce more computerized order-processing flows and reduce the amount of space we need, discussions could open up again. I see no reason why we shouldn't be together in one facility if we could fit and the costs were reasonable.

How about the matter of common clearing with NYMEX or, for that matter, with the Chicago exchanges?

Bowe: Right now there are no active discussions. If the Chicago exchanges get together on common clearing, it is very likely that efforts will be made to merge clearing for all exchanges together, which I would support.

Common clearing is still a goal for the long term. But there are competitive issues that get in the way. Take a look at what happened with the Cotton Exchange products, which had been cleared under a contract with the Chicago Board of Trade. When Cotton announced the Cantor deal, the Chicago Board of Trade said they would not clear those Cotton Exchange contracts. No matter how appealing common clearing is, the exchanges must be protected to be competitive.

My understanding is that in the CBOT-Chicago Mercantile Exchange common clearing initiative, no new exchange can join the common clearing process without the approval of the existing exchanges. It's rather unlikely the CBOT is going to approve the clearance of our Cantor Exchange products. Competitive issues will continue to interfere with common clearing.

Are there other developments on the technology front that will affect trading?

Bowe: We are currently exploring the concept of delivering orders to the broker electronically rather than by paper or voice. I believe we may develop such a system in the next couple of years, either by ourselves for the members or as a joint venture with the members. But that's still in the developmental stage.

You have to remember that the system we currently use for trade-matching and clearing processes is state of the art. In 1991, we put in a new system called TIPS (Trade Input Processing System) that basically interacts with the entire trading process and automates the back end. A computer does the broker-to-broker match to ensure the integrity of the trading process. It simultaneously sends that information to the clearing members for an online acceptance process that feeds the clearing members' own back office systems.

Ever since this system was put in place, we go home at night with less than one-tenth of 1 percent broker-to-broker breaks and less than 1 percent clearing member to clearing member breaks. I don't think any other exchange comes close to those percentages.

When the NYCE decided to harmonize all of its clearing about a year prior to the merger, it put its New York Futures Exchange (NYFE) division trade processing into the CBOT system and took it off TIPS. The members went into an uproar about the inefficiencies of the system. They asked if they could please go back to TIPS, and we reconverted NYFE back to TIPS. With TIPS, the computer is looking for the other side of the trade on a second-by-second basis. The CBOT's batch system goes through the trades every 20 or 30 minutes to see what matches. When you are talking about breaks and errors in volatile markets, 20 minutes becomes an awfully long time.

With the Cotton Exchange bringing its Cantor relationship and Coffee, Sugar & Cocoa adding its technological strength to the deal, the merger seems to benefit both parties. Now, looking at the future of this New York Board of Trade, what direction do you see the exchange going? Is its future in financial products?

Bowe: We will build on our strengths. The deal we have with Cantor Fitzgerald adds interest rate products, which clearly is on the financial side of the business. Once that is up and running, we can broaden the Cantor Exchange products base into any area we deem to be appropriate. We will be working with Cantor, which has a great relationship with its own customer base, to define the next best product to put on the system, particularly once the direct computer-to-computer interface is finalized. Cantor makes it very simple to draw in new products and broaden the network.

If I sound a little vague about new products, it's because I am not going to reveal in a book what those products might be. We'll look at every possible area, and we'll work on those products that have the highest probability of initial success.

One thing I can tell you is that we will continue doing what we have always done. Both the Cotton Exchange and Coffee, Sugar & Cocoa Exchange have a strong tradition of relationships with the trades that use our markets, and we have tried to keep our futures contracts relevant to the commercial use of those commodities. The Cotton Exchange goes back to 1870 and Coffee, Sugar & Cocoa to 1882. Although we try to encourage the growth of the exchange for the benefit of members, we will not lose our focus on the trading communities that rely on us for hedging purposes.

What contracts or product areas are most vulnerable to change or could maybe even disappear? How will your currency contracts, for example, be affected by the Euro?

Bowe: We are deeply involved in those decisions because of our FINEX division, which trades a number of cross-currency rates. Those making a living trading cross-currencies in Europe may have to find something different to do. On the other hand, some of the lesser currencies will be traded more actively because they will be subject to greater focus.

You could see a lot more activity from Eastern Europe as it becomes more active and more industrialized. If you look at history, Eastern Europe used to be the industrial side of Europe and Western Europe the agricultural side. That changed dramatically under communism, but now a rebirth of industry in Eastern Europe may take place as those countries become stronger and make the transition to a free-market system.

One thing the 1990s have shown us is that things that looked unchangeable have now changed. And the speed of change is ever accelerating. Just look at what happened with DTB and the LIFFE in the bund. You see how quickly circumstances can change because you have a few traders who are more facile. The generation behind us is a lot more comfortable with a computer than a pen, and that's the audience that is going to develop what happens next.

The exchanges need to be running in front of the curve and not playing catch-up all the time. I am happy to say that the Board of Trade of the City of New York is positioned better than any other exchange in the United States to benefit from the changes in technology. With the Cantor Exchange, we are going to see very quickly just how well that works.

One item individual traders mention frequently is access to current price quotes and having to pay exchange fees for them. If you don't pay exchange fees, quotes from the New York exchanges are delayed 30 minutes compared to 10-minute delays from other futures exchanges. With the Internet and other technological advances, do you see any changes in the way price quotes and data are disseminated that will benefit the retail trader?

Bowe: In the short term, I don't see significant change. In the longer term, you will definitely see different ways to disseminate prices. At present, we are not in a position with the Internet where we are sufficiently comfortable with security to distribute quotes directly. The security situation will improve and get to the point where exchanges may sell price quotes directly to traders.

But are exchanges likely to put all their real-time quotes online on an Internet site without a charge?

Bowe: It is unlikely we will ever want to freely disseminate prices because there is a significant value to those quotes. The price-discovery function of the futures market is a real asset of the exchanges, and we should be compensated for making price information available.

What is the single most important thing that is going to affect traders and the futures industry in the next five years?

Bowe: Technology and how it's brought to the marketplace will be the crucial issue for the industry, and technology will affect every aspect of our business from order processing to execution services and online risk management.

Over the next few years, technology clearly is going to be the driver behind change in our marketplace. The success of each facet of our business will be directly tied to the use of technology to deliver better service.

CHAPTER

THREE

THE OPTIONS ANGLE

William J. Brodsky
Chairman and Chief Executive Officer
Chicago Board Options Exchange

William J. Brodsky has had an extensive career in the securities and futures industry, ranging from being a runner on the floor of the New York Stock Exchange 35 years ago to brokerage firm attorney to top-level positions at three of the world's major exchanges. His positions included involvement in ground-floor development of both equity options in the 1970s and stock index futures and options in the 1980s.

Brodsky was named chairman and chief executive officer of the Chicago Board Options Exchange (CBOE), the creator of listed options and the world's largest options marketplace, on December 5, 1996, moving back to the securities side of the street after holding top positions at the Chicago Mercantile Exchange (CME) for almost 15 years.

Brodsky began his career as an attorney with the New York investment banking and securities brokerage firm of Model, Roland and Company, where he was one of the first in the securities industry to pass the Registered Options Principal examination. Soon after that, he purchased a membership for his firm on the new CBOE and published a ground-breaking analysis of rules of the newly established CBOE in *The Review of Securities Regulation* in 1973.

25

In 1974 Brodsky moved to the American Stock Exchange (AMEX), where he became head of options trading in 1976 and then executive vice president for operations between 1979 and 1982. For seven years during this period, he was the AMEX representative on the board of the Options Clearing Corporation (OCC), the clearing agent and guarantor of all listed options traded in the United States.

Brodsky was named executive vice president and chief operating officer of the CME in 1982 and three years later was named president and chief executive officer of the CME. A key feature of his CME career was product development, particularly stock index futures and options. Several of the instruments he helped to develop were created in conjunction with the CBOE, including equity derivatives based on the Standard & Poor's indexes, Nasdaq 100 Index, Mexican IPC, S&P 500/ BARRA growth and value indexes, and the Russell 2000 Index. In the aftermath of the 1987 stock market crash, he forged an historic relationship with the CBOE and OCC to provide for cross-margining on futures and options contracts and was instrumental in working with the New York Stock Exchange to establish the system of "circuit breakers" that has helped to manage market volatility.

In addition to his exchange and industry responsibilities, Brodsky serves on a number of educational boards and committees, including the Board of Trustees at his alma mater, Syracuse University, the J.L. Kellogg Graduate School of Management Advisory Council at Northwestern University, and the International Capital Markets Advisory Committee of the Federal Reserve Board of New York as well as a number of charitable and civic committees.

As a top official at both the Chicago Mercantile Exchange and the Chicago Board Options Exchange, you are well acquainted with both the futures and equities sides of trading. How do they compare from a marketing perspective, from a regulatory perspective, from a political perspective?

Brodsky: Let's take them one point at a time. The exchanges have a number of different target markets. The CBOE has made a large commitment to the education of retail investors, with considerable resources allocated to efforts by both the Options Institute and retail marketing departments. In the past, the CBOE has been in a better position to market to retail investors because it has a larger potential sales force of more than 300,000 brokers registered with the Securities and Exchange Commission (SEC) and contracts geared toward the retail investor. Our equity options have done very well in recent years.

Both industries have had strong institutional marketing efforts and have established good contacts with many of the largest institutional investors through efforts such as the annual Risk Management Conference, hosted by the CBOE, CME, Chicago Board of Trade (CBOT) and London International Financial Futures Exchange, calling programs, testimonial advertisements, and videos. A 1997 survey by *Pensions and Investments* noted that 128 pension managers reported using equity or equity index options (Figure 3-1).

The CBOE is initiating a new program to educate high-net-worth investors, and the CBOE has products that are designed to meet the needs of this market.

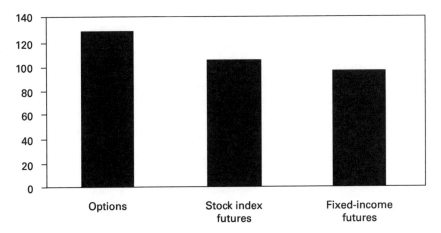

Source: Pensions & Investments survey.

FIGURE 3-1. Number of Pension Managers Using Options or Futures in 1997

As for regulation, the CBOE is regulated, of course, by the SEC, whereas the CME and CBOT are regulated by the Commodity Futures Trading Commission (CFTC). The two regulatory schemes have many similarities but substantial differences.

One reason for these differences is that the SEC approaches its regulatory responsibilities from a concern with disclosure, a full accounting of all factors relevant to a decision to invest in a particular investment. The CFTC, in contrast, begins from a concern with market manipulation.

These different regulatory perspectives may account for the fact that the SEC is staffed primarily with lawyers, whereas the CFTC tends to be staffed with economists. The dissimilar orientation of these two professions obviously influences the thought processes of the two agencies. I should also note that the CFTC's regulation of futures markets tends to be geared to an institutional customer base with the attendant assumption of knowledge and sophistication. The SEC approach to securities markets is geared more to the individual investor and puts much greater responsibility on the broker to establish the suitability of a transaction for a specific customer.

Regarding politics, both the futures and securities markets have a long history of being politically active. The Chicago futures markets are accustomed to working directly with congressional committees charged with oversight of their markets; historically, these committees were very closely involved with the regulation of the commodity futures that were the basis of all the Chicago markets. In contrast, from its inception, the CBOE has worked closely with the SEC, our regulator and most important governmental relationship.

What are the advantages on the securities options side for the retail trader?

Brodsky: The CBOE offers many liquid options on individual stocks and on virtually all the major U.S. stock indexes. For retail investors, the ability to trade both stock and CBOE-listed options from the same account is an advantage over the effort necessary to establish the separate stock and commodities accounts that allow access to futures and futures options.

The CBOE's order-routing, order-handling, and order-trading technology provides faster turnaround time; over 80 percent of all orders arrive at the exchange via our automated routing system.

Options traded on futures exchanges have futures as the underlying instrument rather than the actual stocks or cash value of an index such as the Dow Jones or S&P 500. Futures options, therefore, are more complex products for the average investor. Further, the daily mark-to-market on futures positions may result in large calls for cash even if the overall position is actually hedged by an offsetting position in the stock market.

Rules governing the trading of securities options offer the customer strong protection against the occasional unscrupulous broker. For example, a securities-registered broker who recommends a transaction has an affirmative responsibility to assess the suitability of the trade for the particular customer, in light of the customer's financial situation and investment experience. Further, the risk-disclosure document provided to all securities options customers contains a more detailed explanation of options trading and the risks thereof than does the analogous futures document.

The CBOE's higher degree of market transparency is an advantage for the retail securities options trader. For example, trades of 10 contracts or less are normally eligible for immediate electronic execution on the Retail Automatic Execution System (RAES) against the displayed quote. Thus, what the customer sees on the screen is what the customer gets in the trade.

Further, CBOE's order priority rules also favor retail investors. For example, limit orders go into an order book operated by a CBOE employee. These orders are queued by price and time and have priority over orders represented on the trading floor or those submitted by CBOE market makers. CBOE's firm quote rule, which is the basis for the RAES trades, also assures customers that their orders will be filled at, or better than, the displayed quote when the order arrives at the trading crowd.

CBOE's interactive web site gives customers the opportunity to assess possible outcomes of options trades on a hypothetical basis. The site now attracts more than 20 million hits per month.

What could the futures industry learn from the options industry, or vice versa, that would benefit traders the most?

Brodsky: I believe the options and futures industries have learned quite a bit from each other already. There is a healthy amount of cross-fertilization of ideas here in Chicago because the industries are so interconnected. Securities and futures industry participants learn from each other in the areas of marketing, education, and product innovation, with a resulting gain to the investor.

The CBOE has been the Chicago leader in floor technology and has pioneered order-routing and order-handling systems that may someday be adopted by Chicago's futures exchanges.

The futures exchanges are very competitive and are particularly effective in target marketing to selected segments of the investor community. However, although we are frequent competitors, the exchanges also work together on selected projects—for example, the joint launch of index options and index futures on the Dow Jones Industrial Average and the annual Risk Management Conference I mentioned earlier that is hosted by four exchanges.

What will be the role of index options in the investors' portfolio in the next 5 to 10 years?

Brodsky: Figure 3-2 presents the results of a 1997 survey to determine why institutional investors use equity derivatives. I anticipate that in the next 5 to 10 years stock investors will use index options for many of these same reasons.

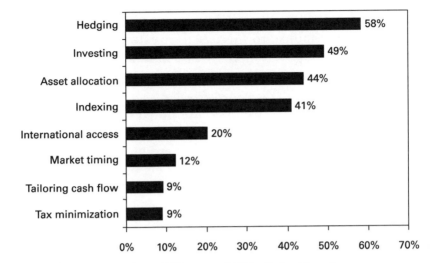

Source: Greenwich Associates: 1997 survey of 147 institutional investors.
FIGURE 3-2.   Reasons That Institutional Investors Use Equity Derivatives

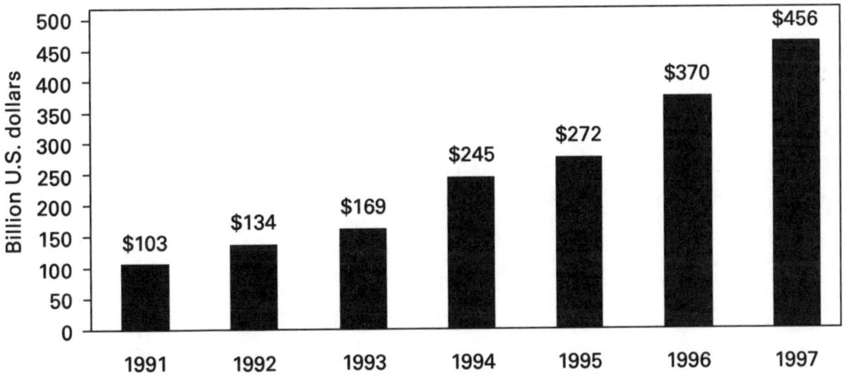

Source: Pensions & Investments.
FIGURE 3-3.   International Assets of Portfolio Managers

An area of continued growth may be international investing and the use of index options on overseas indexes to manage risk as the international assets of portfolio managers and investors grow (Figure 3-3).

What changes or additions in options contracts will be most useful to traders?

Brodsky: In the 1990s the CBOE has been a leader in product innovation. In response to increased investor interest in stock options, the exchange has increased the number of listed classes (underlying stocks) from less than 250 in 1990 to more than 1200 at the end of 1997.

Of equal importance, we have attempted to offer an alternative to the over-the-counter (OTC) market through the listing of FLEX options on both leading index products and individual stocks. FLEX option contracts have elements of both exchange-traded and OTC option products. FLEX offers the benefits of exchange liquidity, an independent daily mark, and the virtual elimination of counterparty risk with OTC advantages of contract customization. FLEX is beneficial to clients who trade large size because FLEX is an alternative to the OTC market, and it also allows the floor trader to compete for business that, historically, has gone to the OTC market.

Finally, our LEAPS products allow investors to benefit from the option risk/return profile but without the restrictions of a short time frame. LEAPS offer the investor the opportunity to benefit from a longer-term outlook on a stock or the market as a whole. This capability removes one of the features of options trading often perceived as a drawback by longer-term investors and has expanded the base of options users.

Most recently, the CBOE has introduced options on the most widely followed U.S. stock market barometer, the Dow Jones averages. Significantly, 40 percent of the open interest in the Dow Jones Industrial Average (DJIA) is in LEAPS, and we intend to continue to innovate and offer more user-friendly products.

Technology has been one of the overriding themes in every business in the 1990s. How will the technology trend affect options trading and traders in the next few years?

Brodsky: Let me start out by describing the actual way in which trading occurs on the CBOE today. First, almost 80 percent of our orders are routed to the exchange electronically. Second, 25 percent of our orders are executed electronically via the Retail Automated Execution System. Third, more than 80 percent of our quotes in the almost 50,000 series we trade are generated electronically out of our AutoQuote system—we disseminate over 3 million quotes every day. Finally, our market-maker handheld terminals and their broker counterparts, the floor broker and mobile floor broker workstations, now report and match more than 60 percent of all trades done on the floor. In fact, overall, paperless transactions now represent more than 80 percent of the CBOE's total trades.

During the next 5 to 10 years, the application of technology to trading-related functions both on and off the trading floor will grow at a very rapid pace. Member firms will utilize technology to improve their market expertise, order-handling and order-execution services, and reporting transactions to the customer. The application of these order-handling and order-execution technologies will reduce the costs of order execution, increase the speed of order turnaround, and enhance market transparency and price discovery. These technologies will make trading increasingly seamless via a PC. I believe we have seen only the tip of the iceberg with respect to the growth of online customer trading.

With increasing investor sophistication, the role of discount firms will continue to grow. These firms have already increased their market share on the CBOE from less than 5 percent in the mid-1980s to more than 15 percent today.

The CBOE has always sought to wed the best of various trading methods with the goal of providing our customers with the best price and most rapid execution. The CBOE will continue to review and modify our trading format to best achieve this goal, which remains our constant touchstone.

How do you think these advances in technology will affect open-outcry trading, traders, and brokers?

Brodsky: As we move into the next century, open-outcry and electronic trading formats will often coexist at the same exchange. Instead of a dichotomy, open-outcry and electronic or automated order-execution systems will be integrated. The CBOE's RAES is an example of this form of integration. Other exchanges will seek to refine or introduce open-outcry/ electronic hybrid trading systems such as the one in use at the CBOE. A hybrid market is able to offer the advantages of both open-outcry and electronic trading formats and, therefore, is the most efficient means of order representation and execution.

Retail traders and brokers will benefit from the enhanced transparency, price discovery, speed, and service brought about as a result of these technologies. Floor traders benefit from the cost savings and ability to handle or participate in a greater number of transactions.

What are the projections for your Dow Jones contract, and how does it fit in with your other contracts?

Brodsky: The CBOE has exclusive rights to the offering of options on the Dow Jones Industrial Average in the United States. We are proud of the fact that the combined open interest in options and LEAPS on the DJIA is more than 600,000 contracts and that the CBOE has a 97 percent share of all broad market index options trading volume on U.S. securities exchanges.

We believe, naturally, that the CBOE is the best place for a customer to invest in index options—the CBOE offers options on more than 40 indexes, including the S&P 100 (OEX), S&P 500 (SPX), DJIA (DJX), Nasdaq 100 (NDX), and the Russell 2000 (RUT). This array of broad-based index options assures a product that will fit any customer's needs.

For example, customers with relatively small portfolios will find the DJX's $8000 to $9000 size appropriate to their needs, whereas customers with larger portfolios may prefer the OEX, at approximately $50,000. Of course, institutional-sized portfolios will probably use the larger SPX, where each contract is worth more than $100,000. Further, the different index products also offer different exercise and expiration features, ranging from the OEX's American exercise with expiration pricing on the close of the market to the SPX's European exercise with expiration based on the opening of the market.

What contracts or markets are most vulnerable to change in the next 5 to 10 years?

Brodsky: All contracts and markets are vulnerable to change in the next 5 to 10 years—change is a constant in our business, and we must be vigilant in trying to stay on the cutting edge.

Open-outcry futures exchanges will see significant changes in the manner in which orders are routed, executed, and processed. Because of the relative simplicity of the futures instrument, the migration toward electronic trading may occur more quickly in futures than for options, which have a very large number of series with many orders involving spreads between different series.

The overall quality of an exchange's integration of technology into its trading system will be an important determinant of its competitiveness. Further, as emerging markets continue to launch exchanges, the futures and options business will become increasingly internationalized.

How will issues such as the Year 2000 (Y2K) computer problems or the Euro currency affect this movement in the next year or so?

Brodsky: Companies' ability or inability to deal with important issues such as Y2K and the European Economic and Monetary Unit (EMU) may affect the prices and volatilities of individual equities and, thus, may affect equity options prices.

The CBOE and the securities industry have taken extensive efforts to assure uninterrupted operation of business as 2000 approaches.

As a result of the EMU, many currency and debt products will be eliminated. However, this development is shifting the focus of European investors toward equity assets and equity derivative products.

Internationally, the EMU may have a significant impact on the now dominant role of the U.S. dollar as the world's reserve currency. If the EMU becomes a rival to the dollar, we may also see trading of non-U.S. stocks on U.S. markets in Euros rather than as dollar-denominated ADRs (American Depositary Receipts).

With all of these things going on, what do you see as the single most important issue or development that will affect traders in the next five years?

Brodsky: Probably the most important driving force will be continued automation and the growth of the Internet as an infrastructure and communication facility open to an enormous global customer base. This will be driven by the demands of customers for fast, low-cost execution. Customers will be the beneficiaries of industry cooperation, consolidation, and technological change as we enter the twenty-first century.

C H A P T E R

F O U R

THE EUROPEAN FRONT

Jörg Franke
Chief Executive Officer
Eurex

Jörg Franke is the chief executive officer of Eurex, the new exchange formed in 1998 by the coming together of the Deutsche Terminbörse GmbH (DTB) and the Swiss Options and Financial Futures Exchange (SOFFEX). He also serves as general manager of FWB Frankfurter Wertpapierbörse (since January 1995) and as a member of the executive board, responsible for the Eurex Division, of Deutsche Börse AG, Frankfurt/Main (since August 1993).

Franke began his career at Westdeutsche Landesbank-Girozentrale, in Düsseldorf, serving in the legal department (1970 to 1973) and securities department (1973 to 1984). He was general manager of the Berlin Stock Exchange from 1984 to 1988 and also was a member of the executive board of Berliner Kassenverein AG-Securities Depository, Berlin, from 1984 to 1989.

Prior to assuming responsibilities for the merged Eurex, he served as chief executive officer of the DTB in Frankfurt from 1988 to 1994 and as general manager of DTB from 1989 to 1998.

As the head of one of the world's major financial exchanges, you have been heavily involved in the develop-

ment and growth of electronic trading. How will futures and options exchanges continue to develop in the next 5 to 10 years?

Franke: As you know, DTB started life as an electronic trading platform and, therefore, has always been completely committed to promoting this type of trading. In this sense, perhaps, we have been fortunate in that we have not had to deal with the change-management process that, for example, Matif (Marché a Terme International de France), our Euro-Alliance partners, or LIFFE (London International Financial Futures Exchange) have had to manage.

However, I think the way forward in the next 5 to 10 years will be dictated by a combination of technological process and the willingness and ability of the worldwide futures and options industry to adapt to the changes that have already begun to take place.

What do these changes mean for the outlook of open-outcry exchanges and floor traders?

Franke: Given my response to the first question, I will have to "sit on the fence" a little bit with my views on what will be the outlook for open-outcry exchanges and floor traders.

On a positive note for electronic trading, we at Eurex have experienced a somewhat surprisingly swift change to automated trading for our D-mark fixed-income products. But we recognize that the Chicago Board of Trade (CBOT), our North American strategic partners, maintains a very successful and efficient open-outcry platform for similar products. On the other hand, we have not been so successful thus far at the short end of the D-mark yield curve, whereas Matif seemed to move the PIBOR (Paris Interbank Offered Rate) business onto its electronic platform very swiftly, and the Euroyen contract at the Tokyo International Financial Futures Exchange has been very successful on screen.

So, to view the scene as certain products being successful on one platform versus another or, ultimately, a complete dominance of screen-based trading versus open-outcry trading in the next five years is difficult to judge, given that there are so many other extenuating factors that complicate the process. However, it is clear that if an open-outcry exchange cannot provide some additional value, it will not survive in the new automated world, as was seen with the Matif's swift transition to screen-based trading.

How will these developments affect the brokerage business in Europe?

Franke: Electronic trading, combined with a zero-cost membership-driven structure, has tended to increase the disintermediation within the business. The associated lack of membership rights and permit agreements has allowed Eurex's membership to proliferate the number of terminals within their organizations but also allowed "end users" to become members in their own right.

What does appear to be certain is that technology will be used to the greatest extent possible to give end users access to the product range as seamlessly as possible. One thing that electronic trading has highlighted is that open-outcry trading is deficient in terms of the overall cost of the "chain process" in ensuring that an order reaches the trading pit and the potential errors that can result from that process.

As a result, the brokerage business generally, not just in Europe, will not be able—or, perhaps, willing—to provide basic execution services. Eurex members have been active in providing their clients with order-routing facilities for such business (including Internet facilities), thereby also giving them greater and quicker access to the market.

In addition, disintermediation has gone a step further with some end users taking membership in their own right. However, this does not mean the complete demise of execution-only brokers because some clients still prefer to leave the responsibility with their broker, although it would seem that only a few will be able to secure enough volume to justify their existence.

Other brokers have already moved on to concentrate on providing "value-added" brokerage services with research capability, etc. But these are likely to be affiliated with larger banking and securities house organizations. In addition, a number of brokerage houses are now happy to sell their clearing and administrative expertise, which, after the Baring's case, has also tended to be linked with selling their superior credit rating.

How will these developments affect the institutional trader? The retail trader?

Franke: The order-routing scenario certainly suggests that the institutional trader will be provided with "virtual" direct access to the market via some form of terminal. In addition, some may determine that it is more cost effective to become direct members of an electronic trading exchange rather than pay a broker who is not providing any value-added services.

Retail traders will probably be supplied with less sophisticated or Internet access to the market (the Chicago Mercantile Exchange's E-mini S&P 500 Index contract, for example), but this, combined with having greater access to information through similar mediums, may give them the comfort to become more active in the markets.

Following the formation of Eurex, what is the outlook for exchange linkages within the European community?

Franke: DTB's merger with SOFFEX to form Eurex was driven by the strategic view that there were too many exchanges in Europe, particularly in a European Economic and Monetary Union (EMU) environment, and that consolidation needed to take place. To achieve the greatest benefit, it would be preferable if this were based on one trading and clearinghouse platform, thereby extracting the greatest synergies for the marketplace. As has been stated on many occasions, the intention is that this type of cooperation is open for all other potential partners that may wish to participate.

Are other international exchange linkages in the works?

Franke: The strategic view that drove the CBOT and Eurex to sign a letter of intent to form a transAtlantic link is that the future of exchange linkages has to be electronically driven. Also, such alliances are more likely to succeed where the partners use the relative strengths of their respective organizations in their own time zones to provide their members with direct access to a wider product range.

In addition, the CBOT and Eurex have stated that they will later attempt to form a tripartite alliance, involving an exchange in the Asian time zone, to complete a 24-hour cycle for those products that justify such listings.

How will these arrangements help traders?

Franke: For the trader this will certainly provide a greater product range on one trading platform. It will also mean that technicians will not be required to provide alternative solutions for different exchanges, and it could ultimately reduce a trader's capital outlay by providing a global cross-margining service across products.

The DTB became a major player in financial markets after launching options and futures in 1990. How do you see Eurex fitting into the world's financial marketplace in the future?

Franke: Rather than elaborate too much on my previous answer, we would like to think that the alliances I have described will place us in a very strong position to further develop our role in the world's financial marketplace. Our continuing progress in what will be Euro-related derivative instruments suggests that we will be Europe's number one futures and options exchange as part of the tripartite alliance described.

In addition to the electronic trading issue, how will the advance of technology generally affect the futures and options industry and traders in Europe in the next five years?

Franke: I have mentioned a number of the technological trends in relation to previous questions so, in that respect, I would like to concentrate here on a different aspect of technology that all exchanges should concern themselves with: The development of the so-called "Proprietary Trading Systems" (PTSs) such as Bloomberg, Instinet (Reuters), and POSIT. They apparently trade more shares than the combined volume of the American Stock Exchange and all regional exchanges, and that provides a technological warning. No exchange has a "right" to maintain their business, and the "first-mover advantage" has been turned into something of a myth by DTB's success in the bund futures business. As a result, exchanges will need to match the technological advancements of their competitors just to stay in the hunt.

If further proof is required, the foreign exchange (FX) business is a prime example. The voice brokers and Reuters dominated this market until the Electronic Brokerage System (EBS), backed by 15 major banking institutions, was set up around five years ago. I believe EBS now represents some 40 percent of the FX brokerage market. Although there may be some other reasons behind this movement than purely technological ones, it is an important lesson for exchanges to note.

How is the Year 2000 (Y2K) issue affecting your exchange?

Franke: DTB addressed the Year 2000 question in a systems release some two years ago by programming the system in such a way that it already believes it is in a later part of the twenty-first century. As such, Eurex has preempted the issue. However, members will still need to program their interfaces to be compatible with this.

How will the new Euro currency affect the futures and options industry and traders?

Franke: We see the introduction of the Euro as a catalyst that has accelerated the changes that would undoubtedly have taken place within the futures and options industry anyway. The European futures and options market will tend to resemble the U.S. marketplace more closely as the proliferation of fixed-income and short-term interest rate contracts consolidate into predominantly one Euro interest rate yield curve. This will challenge volumes in the U.S. Treasury and Eurodollar contracts because the underlying markets will now be of a more comparable size.

What about stock index contracts in the EMU?

Franke: The greatest challenge for the markets will be to develop Pan-European equity index contracts on a scale similar to the existing S&P and Dow Jones contracts in the United States. Eurex's introduction of the STOXX family of futures and options has proved to be very successful when compared to other similar contracts in Europe. Therefore, we are confident we can build on this encouraging start, although the domestic index products such as the DAX in Germany and the SMI in Switzerland are likely to remain important for a number of years to come.

What about the regulatory situation or any other issues related to the EMU?

Franke: It remains to be seen whether EMU itself will ultimately create the changes required to deregulate the European commodities markets, thereby allowing more activity in the agricultural markets and for the energy and metals markets to develop further. Deregulation is being seen in markets such as electricity, but it is too early to determine how such changes may develop.

In addition, the peripheral markets may develop primarily because those traders who are no longer required due to the consolidation in the Euro interest rate and equity markets may be redeployed elsewhere. Taking the FX market as an example, the new cross-trades versus the Central and Eastern European currencies are being traded by ex-D-mark/F-franc traders. As such, countries that are beginning to gear their economies toward EMU entrance criteria will potentially provide the next wave of convergence trades.

What other contracts or markets are most vulnerable to change in the next 5 to 10 years?

Franke: I think my previous comments tend to suggest that all contracts and markets will be vulnerable to change in the next 5 to 10 years. Even where there has already been a great deal of change, it should not be assumed that those markets could not change again. Although the major institutions are still members of a number of different exchanges, they could just as easily switch their short-term allegiances to those exchanges that appear to be the most receptive to their needs. Nobody is in a position to "rest on his or her laurels."

To summarize, what do you see as the single most important futures and options industry issue or development for traders in the next five years?

Franke: Within five years I believe a significant consolidation will have taken place within the markets from Asian, European, and North American perspectives. There will be cross-market trading and clearing, with the U.S. dollar- and Euro-denominated markets driving the changes. To achieve such consolidation, the markets will have to be electronically driven.

What the overall structure will look like and who will be perceived to be the ultimate winners or losers is obviously not certain. However, I believe the relative benefits of an exchange-driven market, compared to the threat of an alternative market formed by well-capitalized financial institutions, will drive the exchanges and clearinghouses to make considerable changes or lose their raison d'être.

BALANCING PAST AND FUTURE

M. Scott Gordon
Chairman of the Board of Directors
Chicago Mercantile Exchange

Scott Gordon, who began his career as a clerk on the exchange floor, was elected chairman of the board of directors of the Chicago Mercantile Exchange (CME) in January 1998. Originally elected to the board in 1982, he has served on the executive committee since 1984 and was vice chairman of the board from 1995 through 1997. He served previously as secretary in 1984, 1985, and 1988 through 1994.

Gordon is executive vice president of Tokyo-Mitsubishi Futures (USA) Inc., a CME clearing member firm owned by the Bank of Tokyo-Mitsubishi Ltd., one of the world's largest financial institutions.

Gordon discovered the fascination of futures markets during a summer job as a clerk on the CME floor in 1971 after his first year of college. Since then, he has been an independent trader, a broker, and a clearing firm executive, trading almost every product type the CME offers and getting insights into the market dynamics of all the CME product groups.

Gordon handled proprietary currency arbitrage for Rosenthal & Company and served as floor manager at the CME and the Chicago Board of Trade (CBOT) for Dellsher Investment Company.

He has been with Tokyo-Mitsubishi and its predecessor firms since 1989. He was a member of the Chicago Board Options Exchange from 1975 until 1977 and the CBOT from 1988 to 1990 and again from 1993 to 1995. He has been a member of the CME's International Monetary Market since 1977.

In addition to his firm and exchange duties, Gordon is also a member of the National Futures Association board and its executive committee and is on the board of the Futures Industry Institute.

You have a broad range of experience at three major Chicago exchanges, and now you are chairman of the Chicago Mercantile Exchange, following in the shoes of such industry stalwarts as Leo Melamed and Jack Sandner. What changes do you see in the direction of the CME in the years ahead that will have the most impact on traders?

Gordon: The industry is changing more rapidly than ever before in our history. The lines have blurred greatly between who is our competitor, member, and customer. Other futures exchanges, once considered our competitors, are now our strategic partners. Cost pressures on futures commission merchants (FCMs) are driving exchanges to promote worldwide industry standardization, and technological developments are finally making it possible to do just that. There is infinitely more information available now at a trader's fingertips.

Traders must familiarize themselves with the latest technological developments, which can actually increase their efficiency while providing them with sophisticated trading tools. The Merc will work diligently to educate our trading population as much as possible and enhance traders' access to technological tools.

The CME is undertaking a comprehensive strategic review of all aspects of the exchange, with the help of a premier consulting firm. Members of the board and our strategic planning committee have been aggressively scheduling meetings exploring potential partnerships in a new global electronic network that we envision to meet our customers' growing demand for more electronic trading. We are moving steadily and deliberately—and quietly—in the right direction. We are making plans for the long term, not responding defensively to perceived short-term threats. But change is occurring rapidly in our industry, and the CME will set its future course expeditiously.

The CME has maintained a balance between the traditional open-outcry pit trading and electronic trading since it submitted its Globex proposal to the Commodity Futures Trading Commission (CFTC) on May 11, 1988. With the advent of a number of electronic trading operations since then, what trends do you see in the way futures trades will be executed in the next 5 to 10 years?

Gordon: As the futures industry faces a period of momentous and rapid change, exchanges worldwide are adapting to cope with a transformed derivatives landscape. The Merc intends to shape the future of global financial risk management. With the completion of our strategic planning effort, we will have significant and bold initiatives to announce for the future.

The CME, of course, was the pioneer in after-hours electronic trading with the introduction of Globex in 1992, and we may have started a trend when we launched the E-mini S&P 500 Index futures and options contracts in September 1997. A smaller version of our benchmark S&P 500 contracts, the E-mini, trades mostly electronically. The fact that it trades adjacent to the larger, open-outcry contracts and benefits from their liquidity clearly contributes to the tremendous success of the E-mini, which has far exceeded our expectations. This clearly is an example of open-outcry and electronic trading complementing each other.

The launch of Globex$_2$, a state-of-the-art system offering traders the ability to fully customize their screens and manage a full range of order types within a Windows environment, puts the CME at the forefront of today's revolution in electronic trading. The Globex$_2$ system's open architecture creates vastly greater opportunities for expanding the reach of our markets to as yet untapped locations as well as for adding new products and markets to the system.

What's become increasingly clear is that 24-hour electronic trading—for certain products—is what our customers want. The CME has made a commitment to create the global electronic network through which customers around the world can access products around the clock. The marketplace will decide the extent to which electronic trading supplants open outcry as the preferred system of trading. One thing that's sure, however, is that the Merc will be strategically positioned to provide access to the global risk management products that our customers demand.

How will these changes continue to affect retail traders and brokers?

Gordon: The most successful traders and brokers will continue to be those who adapt themselves to changing environments. In the case of the E-mini, many traders and customers are able to participate in our electronic trading system through a variety of vehicles we have linked to Globex, including the Internet and our Trade Order Processing System (TOPS).

These changes will obviously have some impact on your floor traders and exchange members. What are the political realities you have to deal with as the exchange chairman and what do they mean for the retail trader?

Gordon: I hope the political realities are invisible to the retail trader and to any exchange customer. We are, of course, a membership organization, and our board is accountable to those members on a daily basis. Members can participate in the future of the exchange by serving on committees and running for election to the board.

As part of the strategic review, we will look at the governance of the institution and our corporate structure to make sure we offer the best value to our members and customers going forward.

You have mentioned your S&P 500 Index contracts and the E-mini as examples of successful trading matching open-outcry and electronic systems. What do you see as the future for stock index contracts in general, and how can traders use Globex to trade this area more effectively?

Gordon: The future of these products is extremely bright, particularly at the CME, which put stock index futures and options on the map and remains the leader worldwide. Products such as the E-mini prove there are always new and innovative products that meet a compelling need.

Many retail traders already have indirect access to Globex through their broker, who can enter orders via Globex, the Internet, TOPS, their firms' proprietary order-routing system, or phone calls to the E-mini pit on our floor.

What are the prospects for Chicago as a futures trading center versus London or Tokyo or some other city in the next 5 to 10 years?

Gordon: It's hard to even imagine that any city other than Chicago could be the futures trading center. Futures trading is an important part of Chicago's culture, and I don't foresee that changing. The CME, more than 25 years ago, established itself as the first truly global marketplace, and we remain a global institution to this day. We will continue to attract new customers from all over the world as we redefine the concept of risk management.

One of the issues in this regard involves common clearing. What would common clearing offer to the futures industry, brokerage firms, and traders?

Gordon: Common clearing will be a positive development for the industry, firms, and traders, achieving efficiencies and eliminating unnecessary duplications. In March 1998, the CME, the CBOT, and the Futures Industry Association signed a letter of intent on common clearing, coming to an agreement on many issues that had seemed insurmountable in the past. I remain hopeful that in 1999 we will implement this important initiative (following membership approval in a referendum at both exchanges).

Technology has been a major influence on business. In addition to electronic trading, how do you think advances in technology will affect the futures industry and traders in the next few years?

Gordon: The technological evolution already has had a tremendous impact on us, enabling us to increase efficiency and the speed with which orders are entered, reported, and confirmed. Similarly, it has quickened the delivery of news and information to traders both on and off the trading floors. It has brought electronic trading and opened up our markets to give traders and customers access to our markets around the clock.

The Merc has worked hard to ensure that our exchange and member firms are well prepared for Year 2000 conversion issues on all technological fronts. Technological developments have contributed to a state-of-the-art clearing system, CLEARING 21, which we developed in concert with the New York Mercantile Exchange.

No doubt technology will have a tremendous impact on the industry, this exchange, and traders in the coming years, and we are only beginning to imagine the ways in which it will do so.

How will the new European currency affect the CME, the futures industry, and traders?

Gordon: In May 1998 the CME launched ECU futures and options—that is, contracts based on the European Currency Unit, a basket of 25 currencies. These contracts will convert directly to Euro futures and options on January 1, 1999, when European Economic and Monetary Union (EMU) is scheduled to take effect.

The only CME contracts directly affected by the EMU are futures and options on the Deutsche mark and the French franc. For a period of time, these currency products will continue to trade on the CME, concurrent with the ECU or Euro contracts, until the D-mark and franc currencies disappear.

What other markets are most vulnerable to change in the next 5 to 10 years?

Gordon: I wish I had a crystal ball. I think it is clear, however, that all markets are susceptible to extraordinary change and that we must remain flexible, nimble, and open-minded to make the most out of that change.

To summarize, what will be the single most important futures industry issue or development for traders in the next five years?

Gordon: I believe that among the greatest issues traders will face are how to make the most of technological developments and how to manage the flow of information to ensure that they are effectively using all the data and news available to them to make the best trading decisions while not experiencing the phenomenon known as "information overload."

CHAPTER

S I X

EDUCATING THE TRADER

Joel Greenberg
President
Alaron Trading Corporation

Joel Greenberg has been an active leader in the brokerage business and at the Chicago Mercantile Exchange (CME) for more than 30 years. He is president of Alaron Trading Corporation, a full-service futures commission merchant offering retail, discount, and managed futures brokerage services.

Greenberg began his career in sales and software systems design with both RCA and General Electric. From 1969 to 1986 he was vice president of Heinold Commodities Inc., and from 1987 to 1989 he was vice president of Shearson Lehman before joining Alaron, a firm started and run by his three children.

A member of the CME since 1967, Greenberg served as a CME director in 1976 to 1979 and 1996 to 1997, including service as first and second vice chairman. He has served as either the chairman or member of numerous exchange committees, including Live Cattle, Feeder Cattle, New Products, Live Hogs, Pork Products, Agricultural Oversight, Public Relations, and ClearinghOuse. He was a founding member of the Political Action Committee and served on many ad hoc committees related to new products and CME internal expansion.

He is also a past member of the International Monetary Market and Index and Options Market at the CME and the Chicago Board of Trade.

Greenberg also serves on several corporate boards and has been a director on several hospital boards as well as the Weizmann Institute of Science and Chicago Israel Bonds.

You have seen the brokerage business evolve over many years, and now technology is producing some rapid changes in how you do business. How is the major role of today's brokerage firm changing, and how is technology influencing your operation?

Greenberg: Probably the single most important aspect for the retail trade will be the education of the retail trader—what to look for and what to do. Many traders have gone to the technical approach to trading rather than fundamentals. But, with the advent of electronic order placement and the ability to get information on the screen out to everybody at the same time, I think fundamentals will play a much more important part in the individual's trading.

It's going to be the task of the brokerage firm to educate the traders about what to look for and how to take advantage of certain developments that come along in various commodities. Everybody realizes that the instantaneous order fill from electronic trading is going to be like a game for some people—like the slot machine magnified. It is going to attract a much greater retail audience. I think it will be easier for firms to handle the retail business, but they will need to help these newcomers.

Brokerage firms are going to have to step up their ability to make sure that online trading is adaptable to preserve the security of the company—that is, when a customer enters an order, it is going to have to be checked against the customer's risk management profile before the order flows to the floor. All that will be instantaneous and in real time. That technology is in place, but it will have to continue to develop.

We are using systems like TOPS (the CME's Trade Order Processing System for entering orders), but the end of TOPS, which is CUBS (CME Universal Broker Station), has really not done the job, even though we have spent literally millions on it. It's cumbersome for the broker; that will have to be advanced.

To sum up the impact of technology on firms such as ours, I think the use of new technology will be positive for the broker-age firms and positive for our ability to attract more retail busi-ness. Our biggest job will be education.

How will this technology affect the "traditional" broker role in the years ahead?

Greenberg: Average traders at home will not have to rely on a broker in the same way as in the past because they will have on their own screen the same information the broker has. The trader just has to know where to get it. As new people begin trad-ing, there will have to be some hand-holding, of course, and bro-kers will still have to be interpreters of data and information as well as order handlers.

We tell our brokers to really specialize in one or two com-modities and be the king of that area. They obviously have to know about every area, but you get a lot more respect from cli-ents if you really know a lot about a couple of commodities. You are the expert. I think it works that way in the medical field, too—everybody understands the general practitioner, but where do they go when they need real help? To the specialist.

Looking at the exchange angle, what is the effect of technology on the floor trader? What is the outlook for the open-outcry setting and exchanges?

Greenberg: I think open outcry has a chance to last longer in agricultural commodities than in any other field. In the ag mar-kets in particular, I can see open outcry working side by side with electronic trading.

The exchanges really have a job to do—my experience is with the CME, but I am talking about the exchanges in general. The exchanges have talked about strategic planning for a long time, but they had other things on their minds and only gave it lip service. Well, now they are really turning their attention to a strategic plan, probably more out of necessity than anything.

What the exchanges need to do is figure out (1) where the revenue streams are going to be and (2) a way for memberships to still have value. I will get disagreements on this, but I think the floor broker is going to have a much diminished role in the business. The exchanges may be able to set up a way for these brokers to participate in the flow of orders—I don't have a way, but maybe they could verify trades and get a commission for that. Who knows what could develop?

But the exchanges themselves have to identify their revenue streams, and the floor brokers will have to change their mode of operation.

We'll come back to floor traders in a minute, but one issue along this line for exchanges involves vendors and traders having to pay exchange fees for real-time quotes. Do you see any changes in this practice?

Greenberg: Sure, it will change. First, you have to realize the exchanges get a tremendous amount of revenue from quote distribution. Maybe, in addition to quotes, we tag on something else that is worth money to whomever wants it.

Real-time volume and open interest figures, for example?

Greenberg: I think one of the things that would be important to know is whether the trade that is taking place is a commercial trade or a retail trade—a real-time Commitment of Traders report. That's the type of thing that technology might bring.

Let's come back to your brokerage hat. As trading becomes more global, how will brokerage firms such as yours deal with 24-hour trading?

Greenberg: This trading tends to be more in indexes than in physical products. It's very difficult, for example, to trade hogs around the clock, as you can well imagine, when there is no cash trading going on. You could wake up in the morning and find that someone in Asia, for example, has decided to put the price way out of line for our opening. I even see that in the S&P. Sometimes I see the market, say, 600 points out of line one minute before our open and the next tick it's 200 points. That won't go over big with farmers.

What global trading does do is that brokerage firms will have to have online updating to validate a customer's position and ability to trade at all times. We have already seen instances where someone will try to enter a five-car order in the S&P and we take that order. Then, if that customer adds another five and another five during a certain time frame, we may not pick up the overexposure, whereas if it had been a 15-car order, we would catch that right away. We will have to have real strict abilities to monitor clients.

We already maintain a staff all night, 24 hours a day, and on weekends. We get plenty of calls on the weekend.

You have mentioned education and the flow of information as important facets of the brokerage business in the future. How will brokerage firms help traders in these areas? Are we at the end of the once-a-week newsletter era?

Greenberg: I think it will be a combination of things. Each company will have its own web site, as many already do, and the information will have to be updated as close to real time as possible—almost like having a wire service over the Internet. The government may put out a flat statement about some transaction or another, and traders might have to go to the broker's Internet site to find out the significance of the deal.

Some analysis will be free to attract customers, such as excerpts from our newsletters that are on the web site, but some things that have more value, such as a complete research report, may have a fee involved. The more information and the better the information online, the more likely you are to attract an account to your firm and get the retail business. I think that's the goal of most brokerage web sites now.

And there will be specialty companies. Alaron is involved in trading all markets but has a very strong agricultural base; other companies are more financially oriented. There may also be more specialty information services.

How will you teach traders to trade better?

Greenberg: We really don't "teach" traders to trade, and they may not learn how to trade any better unless they become a professional in the commodity they are trading. But if we can give them more updated information and potential strategies for trading a market, it will make them think they are trading better and with more knowledge.

Essentially what it comes down to is a perception. You may have the same information at the same time everybody else has it, but it is how you perceive what it means to the marketplace that is important. Our job is to convince that retail client out there that he or she is as sharp now as any professional in the business—psychology 101. It comes down to education, psychology, and the tools you offer to enhance that education.

Right now many investors have a lot of money from the stock market—or at least they have the perception they are a lot wealthier now than they were three years ago. In this type of situation, they feel they can do a few extra things with it, and one of them could be to trade futures.

Yes, more people do have sizable portfolios from 401k plans or mutual funds. They haven't cashed in on them yet, but they do have the feeling they are better off. If (or when) the stock market turns, where will these people come into futures markets? In the ag commodities? Financials? Currencies?

Greenberg: I happen to think that agriculture is interesting for the future because I think we are becoming more international in our trading of ag products. The grain markets have had this influence for years but not the meat markets. I envision—and we have done some research into it—that we will have regional meat indexes, such as a Far Eastern meat index, a European meat index, or a North American meat index with arbitrage between regions. That could be very big.

The future in futures is going to be in indexes more than in the products—international indexes that reflect different areas of the world. You can't invent a pork belly or a ham, but when you put the indexes together, they offer some opportunities. They are a lot easier for people to understand. The tough thing is getting the right items in the index and getting the prices verified.

As an ag-oriented firm, how do you view the proposals for a two-tier marketplace or for off-exchange markets for agricultural commodities?

Greenberg: First, I do not favor two-tier markets. Period. Institutional brokers might like their own little market, but the best argument for having all trading in one market is easy: It works.

The two-tier question, of course, also relates to off-exchange options. I think they should be regulated. When somebody comes up with a colossal lawsuit because somebody forfeited on a contract, you'll see a little different feeling from the Commodity Futures Trading Commission. I believe everybody has a right to enter into a business transaction, and if people want to do options off the exchange, fine. But they should be regulated.

The cooperatives and the warehouses that store the grain apparently want to make their own individual deals. But all you have to do is look at some experiences with the hedge-to-arrive contracts a year or two ago to see the potential for problems in an unregulated setting.

What is your view of other nonexchange markets such as what Cantor Fitzgerald is doing or of some screen-based entity that wants to trade the Euro and other currencies, for example?

Greenberg: If Cantor Fitzgerald can cause the kind of ripples of anxiety that it has in the Treasury market at the Chicago Board of Trade (CBOT), the same thing could happen in other markets as well. The Euro could be a perfect screen-traded product for institutions.

The strength the current exchanges have, of course, is their clearing ability and standing behind all the trades. The problem with a Cantor Fitzgerald or a combination of an XYZ and ABC, as big as they could be, is that there is still a chance that something could go wrong; who is going to back them up? As it stands now, that's the saving grace of the exchanges. They have the confidence of the marketplace.

Now that you have your exchange hat on, how do you picture the trading floor of the future in the face of challenges from electronic trading and other exchange-type bodies? Will there still be a floor in five years?

Greenberg: That's a good question. It won't be the same. If the market moves to electronic trading, it probably would be preferable for floor traders to have one gigantic floor and 700 or 1000 screens, with an ag area, a financial area, etc.—like the E-mini trades today. It would give the right kind of flavor to have them together. That might be one alternative.

I think the CBOT made a humongous mistake when it built its financial floor. I told my kids when the CBOT was going after the Dow Jones contract that it was going to be a failure because the institutions don't trade 30 or 65 stocks; they trade the stocks in S&P 500, the bigger index. I said then that, two years from now, the price of a CBOT seat will be under the price of a CME seat. I didn't think our (CME) price was going to go so low, but the CBOT seat price would be there if not for the value of the Chicago Board Options Exchange seat. With $200 million in debt, the CBOT seat will go lower.

I don't know the end result for floor trading, but I do think there will be only one master electronic trading system, something like Globex$_2$. I can't see the need to have so many different electronic systems.

If you need only one electronic trading system, would that suggest a move to common clearing by the Chicago exchanges?

Greenberg: Here is something you would think should be a fairly open-and-shut case. It makes a lot of sense. In fact, a merger makes better sense—put all the agricultural contracts on one floor and all the financials on another. That would seem like a feasible thing to do.

But there are some people at the exchange—I don't want to name names here—who can't fathom why the CME would want to give up owning 100 percent of a clearinghouse to own 24 percent of a clearinghouse and why the CME should bail out the futures commission merchants (FCMs) and the CBOT. One suggestion was, if anything, do a deal with the FCMs and leave the CBOT out of it. So there is plenty of opposition to common clearing. If some key people are against it, common clearing is going to be a very tough sell.

What about another idea that has been floating around—the possibility the CME will move from member to public ownership?

Greenberg: There has been a lot of talk about that. If we could figure out a way to do it, I think we could go that route. We have been looking at the structure of the membership, but any change is fraught with a lot of problems, politically and economically. If we could pay out something of a dividend to members now—at least, get people into the frame of mind of a for-profit setup—it would make it a lot easier to make the next move, even if there are tax consequences initially.

Coming back to the brokerage side of things where you earn your livelihood, how will the brokerage business fare in all this?

Greenberg: I see a lot of electronic clouds out there, but once you break into the clear, it could be great. The FCM off-floor brokerage end of the business will do well. The Merrill Lynches, the Dean Witters, the Baches . . ., they hurt themselves. They could correct this quickly, but they wrapped themselves into the institutional world where they can't make any money. For them, the retail is too dangerous because of the lawsuits and time requirements; the institutional isn't profitable because they have to fight for competitive advantage.

That's opened the door for companies like Alaron. A few of us are doing well serving retail customers.

Do you have any final thoughts on how you envision the future of trading?

Greenberg: I have been doing a lot of thinking about what the future would look like in the next few years. The technology, I think, is basically here for what I envision, and that is virtual on-line trading. In this visionary world, I could get on the Internet and see a trading pit—or a virtual pit—with you on the other side, and I could actually hear you say you have five to sell at a price and I could electronically buy that five and maybe sell you five more.

In that setup, we could still own memberships and trade electronically from wherever we are in the world. A lot of things would have to be done to implement such a system, of course, but I think the basic technology is available, such as being able to see one another on the Internet.

We must acknowledge that electronic trading is here. The question is how best can we marry the electronic and open-outcry systems. The best way to do it—we'll call it fantasy land—may be virtual online trading. I'm not quite sure how to get there, but this is an idea.

What we need to do is to get a bunch of industry people together in small groups in some kind of strategic planning retreat and toss all of these crazy ideas out and see what sticks. If everybody gets a chance to express ideas, who knows what we might come up with?

C H A P T E R

S E V E N

WINDOW TO CHINA

William D. Grossman
General Counsel
Hong Kong Futures Exchange

William D. Grossman, general counsel of the Hong Kong Futures Exchange Ltd. (HKFE) since December 1997, has been involved in Far East markets for a number of years, both as a representative of the Chicago Board of Trade and in positions with several firms in Hong Kong.

After spending the first four years of his career at the Commodity Futures Trading Commission as associate director of the Division of Trading and Markets and legal counsel to Commissioner David Gartner, Grossman joined the Chicago Board of Trade (CBOT) in 1981. At the CBOT he was vice president and associate general counsel, 1981 to 1984; an independent floor trader, 1984 to 1985; director of international market development, 1985 to 1988; vice president/managing director, Asia-Pacific Representative Office in Tokyo, 1988 to 1992; and vice president of international relations, 1992 to 1993.

Grossman moved to Quantum Financial Services (Hong Kong) Ltd. as Chief Representative-Asia from December 1993 to December 1994, Cargill Investor Services (Hong Kong) Ltd. as Senior Representative-China from January 1995 to March 1996, and Jardine Fleming Futures Ltd. as director from March 1996 to November 1997 prior to joining the HKFE.

A member of the HKFE board of directors since June 1997, Grossman has also served as a consultant or advisor to several World Bank programs and committees related to futures trading in the People's Republic of China.

Your area of the world has experienced some tremendous changes politically and economically in recent years, perhaps more so at your exchange than with any other exchange, so we need to start with the big picture.

Grossman: The two most significant events in the futures industry in this region, of course, have been (1) the rise and fall of the futures industry in the Peoples Republic of China (P.R.C.) and (2) the Asian financial market turmoil beginning in 1997.

In China, the futures industry grew from nothing in 1989 to a sprawling mass of more than 40 exchanges and 500 brokerage firms by 1994. In the absence of effective regulation and efficient banking services, abuses became rampant. In 1994 the central government began a rectification program that included a ban on trading in overseas futures markets, the elimination of more than half the brokerage firms, and a reduction in the number of futures exchanges to 15. It is expected that the number of exchanges will be reduced further, to about three or four, and within the next two years, at last, a national futures law will be enacted.

What do these developments suggest for the role of futures in China?

Grossman: This experience vividly demonstrates the latent demand for risk-shifting instruments in the world's most populous country and the absolute necessity for effective regulation as a condition to the success of any derivatives market. Will China become a force in world derivatives markets? Definitely, yes. When will this happen? Not until after 2000.

How have the recent financial fluctuations affected futures trading?

Grossman: The recent financial turmoil in Asia bolstered the standing and reputations of futures exchanges in the region that exercise strict risk management and self-regulation. Although it was a novel experience for some to see futures prices move more quickly and dramatically than cash prices, the realization soon took hold that futures were not moving the cash market but, instead, were just communicating the market's opinion about cash market value more efficiently than the cash market. Already, as many markets in the region are beginning to recover, investors are returning first to the markets that let them out the easiest.

How has the Hong Kong Futures Exchange fared in this recent turmoil, and what changes have been made to facilitate trading or attract traders?

Grossman: The recent success of the Hong Kong Futures Exchange can be attributed to its strict and effective risk management procedures. The exchange, of course, has no control over volatility, which is the primary catalyst for volume, but it does control the soundness of the clearing function and the common bond system. Its risk management procedures have earned the confidence of fund managers and corporate treasurers, and this has provided the foundation for the exchange's steady progress.

The next growth phase will be spurred by the introduction of regional interest rate, stock index, and currency contracts as well as the migration of trading from open outcry to an electronic environment.

Looking at this regional emphasis and considering the competition in the Asian time zone, why and how should Hong Kong fit into the global traders' portfolio in the next 5 to 10 years?

Grossman: Hong Kong is, and will continue to be in the foreseeable future, the most efficient location to raise capital, invest, and manage risk related to the development of the Greater China region, including the Peoples Republic of China, Taiwan, and Hong Kong. Despite the promising prospects for futures markets in the Peoples Republic of China, it will be many years before both actual risk management procedures and the reputation for effective risk management can approach levels that have been achieved in Hong Kong. For the next 5 to 10 years, anyone who needs to hedge China financial risk will come to Hong Kong.

In addition, Hong Kong is known for its modern and efficient regulatory and banking systems. If traders or fund managers have a choice of trading comparable products in other Asian jurisdictions, which may have foreign exchange controls, excessive reporting requirements, or position limits on foreigners, or in Hong Kong, which has none of these, they will undoubtedly choose Hong Kong. This, along with the China advantage, is the Hong Kong edge that will become increasingly apparent in the next 5 to 10 years.

Let's talk a little more about China. What impact will China have on trading in Hong Kong or, for that matter, on other exchanges around the world?

Grossman: As mentioned earlier, China will have a significant impact on futures trading around the world, particularly in Hong Kong, during the next 5 to 10 years. The short but tumultuous history of futures trading in China yields one unmistakable conclusion: The Chinese are wonderful customers. The jury is still out, however, on the ability of China to manage and regulate markets. If this pattern holds, there will be surplus demand for futures trading that will spill over China's borders and land primarily in Hong Kong but also in other markets around the world.

This trend will be compounded by the commercialization and internationalization of the banking and trade sectors in

China, which will stimulate further demand for risk-shifting vehicles. Although computerization will have the most significant impact on the cost side of the futures industry in the next 5 to 10 years, demand from China will have the single most significant impact on the revenue side.

You indicated that electronic trading would be a factor in the Hong Kong Futures Exchange's next growth spurt. How do you see this development affecting futures and options exchanges in general and the HKFE specifically in the next few years?

Grossman: The golden age of product innovation in the futures industry is past. The new golden age belongs to systems development. Although there will surely continue to be new products developed, the driving force in the industry will be the electronic delivery of services to brokers and customers. What T-bonds, the S&P, and Eurodollars did for the futures industry in the 1980s, the computer and Internet will do in the next century.

Accordingly, the development plans of the HKFE in the next few years will feature a migration of all trading to an automated format. This initiative is driven by one factor in particular: cost. There are legitimate differences of opinion about whether greater liquidity can be developed on the screen or on the floor. The consensus in Hong Kong, however, is that, even if the floor might provide a little greater liquidity, it is not worth the cost to member firms or to the exchange itself.

It is safe to say that in Asia all new futures exchanges will be launched on electronic platforms and that the extent of open-outcry trading has passed its peak.

For the HKFE, in addition to the migration of open-outcry trading to an electronic platform, the focus during the next 5 to 10 years will be to introduce regional interest rates, currency, and stock index products, with a particular emphasis on serving the China market.

How will these developments affect the institutional trader? The retail trader?

Grossman: The objective of systems and product development initiatives at the HKFE and other exchanges is to provide more comprehensive, cost-effective, and financially secure risk management and investment services to both institutional and retail traders. As information and trade execution capabilities become increasingly automated and distributed via mass communication media such as the Internet, the value of brokers' advisory and trade execution services will diminish.

Technology will, in effect, disintermediate a major historical component of the brokerage business. What institutional and retail customers eventually will pay their intermediaries for is advice, bookkeeping, and financial integrity. What exchanges and their clearinghouses will have to provide institutional and retail investors—and their brokers—are economies of scale in complementary product offerings, such as coverage of an entire currency yield curve or coverage of regional equity indexes or debt securities—and, again, financial integrity.

In this changing environment, what is the outlook for international exchange linkages?

Grossman: Exchanges that pursue product linkages may have their eyes set on the future, but their feet would appear to be firmly rooted in the past. An exchange can deliver products around the world through automated systems without the need to link with other exchanges.

On the other hand, exchanges that pursue clearing linkages to achieve cost and operational efficiencies in trade processing and the optimal use of their own and members' capital are on the cusp of the next dominating trend in the futures industry. The mutual offset between the Chicago Mercantile Exchange and the Singapore International Monetary Exchange had its place on the stage of futures industry history. Tomorrow's acts will follow the script of London Clearing House and Chicago Common Clearing.

Technology has gradually peeled away the outer layers of the exchange service package to reveal the essential inner core, which is clearing. When a firm had to set up a booth and a floor team at an exchange, the exchange could compete in terms of cost and efficiency. As part of this process, exchanges developed their own identity and personality, which also were used to distinguish themselves from the competition. But technology is taking away most vestiges of the distinctive "brand" value of exchanges and making them more generic instead. The result is that, in a few years' time, the same product traded on different exchanges will be virtually indistinguishable—except for one factor: clearing.

This trend should not dilute the incentive for exchanges to create new products but should provide a salutary boost for the further improvement of clearing and risk management systems. The result for traders will be a more secure environment in which to invest or manage risk.

In addition to electronic trading, how do you see the technology trend affecting futures and options brokers and individual traders?

Grossman: Basically, the advance of technology and the increasingly widespread use of the Internet have the potential to disintermediate aspects of the brokerage function and put exchanges in competition with their members for at least the order-entry services currently provided by brokers. In addition, to the extent that nonclearing member institutional traders can meet applicable financial requirements, the efficiencies provided by automation could make it more economical for them to become clearing members themselves.

What contracts or markets are most vulnerable to change in the next 5 to 10 years?

Grossman: The economic emergence of China and India has the potential to revolutionize supply and demand patterns for key agricultural and industrial commodities, which would have attendant effects on futures markets. It is difficult to predict exactly how this would play out, but the two most likely ramifications would be the "internationalization" of contract specifications for existing agricultural and industrial commodity futures and/or competition from emerging-market Asian exchanges.

To summarize, what do you see as the single most important futures and options industry issue or development for traders in the next five years?

Grossman: The single most important issue for traders in the next five years will be the proliferation of electronic order-entry and execution systems. Traders will need to adjust not only to the new order-entry and execution methodologies but also to the new "personality" of the electronic marketplace. During the next five years, new products will consist mainly of variations on existing themes. The action will take place on the systems side.

LEAVING A VISION

Hal T. Hansen
Former President
Cargill Investor Services Inc.

Hal T. Hansen has been one of the most influential leaders in the futures and options industry, holding the most prestigious positions in the industry prior to his retirement on July 31, 1998. He says his comments about the Chicago exchanges in this chapter are "really my last piece of advice to the Chicago exchanges. . . . I am extremely concerned about the viability of both Chicago exchanges unless aggressive, dramatic action is taken in the very near future."

Hansen served as chairman of both the Futures Industry Association (FIA) from 1992 to 1994 and the National Futures Association (NFA) from 1994 to 1998. A director of both groups since 1982, he also was a member of the executive committees of both for a number of years and chaired a number of key committees including the Membership Committee and the Finance Committee of the NFA and the Financial Integrity Task Force of the FIA.

A native of Kansas, Hansen spent his entire 40-year career with one firm, Cargill Inc. and subsidiaries, starting with the Commodity Marketing Division as a merchant and branch manager in 1958. His other stops included director, Cargill S.A. in Buenos Aires, 1965 to 1969; assistant manager, Poultry Products and International Feed Departments, 1970 to 1971; general manager, Paramount Poultry Division, 1971 to 1974; vice president and regional manager, C.I.S., Atlanta, 1974 to 1978; and then president of Cargill Investor Services Inc. for 20 years from 1978 until he retired in 1998.

A member of both the Chicago Board of Trade (CBOT) and the Chicago Mercantile Exchange (CME) since 1978, Hansen served as a director of the CBOT from 1987 to 1990 and was a member of the futures commission merchant (FCM) committees at both exchanges during the 1990s. He also served on or chaired a number of other committees at the exchanges and was a member of the Commodity Futures Trading Commission (CFTC) Regulatory Coordination Advisory Committee from 1990 to 1996.

In addition to the Chicago exchanges, he is a member of the Kansas City Board of Trade, Minneapolis Grain Exchange, and Winnipeg Commodity Exchange. He was chairman of the Futures Committee of the National Broiler Council, 1980 to 1984, and president of Delmarva Poultry Industries Inc., 1973 to 1974.

You were actively involved in developing the U.S. futures industry for more than 20 years. Now, with the wisdom and insight you have gained as you leave the day-to-day activity behind, what changes do you see ahead for the structure of the industry?

Hansen: First of all, it is necessary to make an outline to quantify as nearly as possible what structural changes we anticipate will occur in this time frame.

The easiest changes to predict are

1. Computerization of the industry.
   a. Totally electronic processes (most financial instrument markets, such as Eurex).
   b. Electronically enhanced open outcry (certain physical markets such as grains at the CBOT, livestock at the

CME, energy/metals at the New York Mercantile Exchange/Commodity Exchange (NYMEX/Comex), metals at the London Metal Exchange).

    c. Order routing (Internet versus dedicated networks such as Globex/NSC, Market Power/DTB, APT II, proprietary firm systems).

    d. Back-office systems, which will manage and communicate account information.

2. Alliances and mergers

    a. Common clearing (CBOT/Eurex, CME with London International Financial Futures Exchange (LIFFE) and the Singapore International Monetary Exchange, and other pairings)

    b. Here's a wild card: Merger of the CBOT and CME

    c. Further consolidation of financial institutions, including FCMs

3. Consequences of European Economic and Monetary Union (and other regional economic unions)

The more difficult changes to predict include

1. Regulatory consolidation.

    a. CFTC merger into the Securities and Exchange Commission?

    b. Global regulatory alignment.

2. Product development, basically exchanges versus over-the-counter operations.

    a. Who will be the survivors from the twentieth century?

    b. New products for the next millenium.

3. Customers: Who will be in? Who will be out?

    a. Retail customers. Who will they be? Who will handle this category of trading?

    b. Institutional customers. This needs further segmentation.

       (1) Bank and investment company proprietary trading.

(2) Pension, trust fund, endowment internal money managers, proprietary hedging.
(3) Pension, trust, endowment third-party money managers.
(4) Hedge funds.
(5) Futures funds.
(6) Professional traders, nonexchange.
(7) Professional traders, exchange.

c. Commercial customers, the "basic" risk managers. These include agricultural producers, processors, merchants; industrial producers, processors, traders; energy producers, marketers, traders.

How will all of these changes affect retail and institutional traders?

Hansen: Not to dodge the question, but that outline of variables and complexities clearly demonstrates there are no simple answers. However, some general conclusions can be drawn about how traders, both retail and institutional, will be affected by all of this:

1. All order-entry and execution processes will migrate to computer screen-based mechanisms. "Phoning orders to the floor" or calling a broker will be cost-prohibitive and too slow.
2. Financial instruments in organized, centrally cleared, exchange markets will all be screen-traded. Here, cash and futures are fully fungible.
3. Futures and options contract markets based on "physical" products (grains, livestock, energy, metals) will endure at least 10 years in computer-enhanced, open-outcry environments. Here, cash markets are generally not fully fungible with futures.
4. Institutional and commercial clients will have trading terminals linked directly to the exchanges and will be cleared and administered through FCM intermediaries.

5. Retail trading will be done over the Internet, subject to regulatory oversight similar to what exists today and cleared by firms specializing in this segment.

6. Locals (floor traders) in financial contracts will have opportunities to continue their market-making role but will have to adapt to computer trading. Those involved in physical products will continue in an open-outcry environment but will have to adapt to computerized processes for needed efficiencies.

7. Floor brokers in financial instruments will find their function migrating to computers, whereas brokers in physical markets can continue their role, at least for several years, if they embrace computerized order-handling processes.

8. All customers will receive their trading information, confirmations, margin calls, account administration, etc., via interactive computer processes. They will be able to access their account information directly via the Internet or a dedicated link to their clearing firm.

9. Futures exchanges will adapt to all of the above in various ways.

That is quite an outline. First, let's talk a little about the segmentation of customers you mentioned several times and the proposals for a "two-tier market." What are the pros and cons for a two-tier setup with two sets of regulations, one for the retail trader and one for the institutional and commercial trader?

Hansen: Let's clear up a common misunderstanding when the term "two-tier" is used. The concept of two-tier markets generally refers to the "professional market" proposals that have been floated in recent years. The primary objective of these proposals is to relieve the professional and institutional and commercial traders, and the organized markets in which they trade, from burdensome regulatory oversight and intervention. These markets would trade separately, albeit parallel, to the more heavily regulated "retail" markets.

Alternately, there is the concept of two-tier regulation that refers to a regulatory process that clearly recognizes the differences between "sophisticated" professional market participants and the "public" or "retail" customers, who are deemed to be more susceptible to fraud, misrepresentation, and other perceived evils of the futures industry. Here, the market remains the same, but the participants are regulated in a totally distinct way.

In my view, the notion of two-tier markets is impractical, costly to maintain, and really not necessary in the computerized environment of the future. Furthermore, this structure would be noncompetitive with the emerging electronic exchange powerhouses such as Eurex. Do you ever hear of the European or Asian exchanges talking about two-tier markets? Certainly not.

The challenge rests in how our existing markets—and anticipated markets in the future—are regulated. The focus has to be on achieving a rational and workable regulatory scheme that recognizes the sharp distinctions between professional and retail market participants.

Our current regulatory structure is an archaic legacy from the 1930s that has failed to evolve as markets and participants have changed dramatically. It is due a total overhaul, including instituting processes that clearly recognize the differences between professional participants and those who need a higher level of regulatory protection. Every major regulatory jurisdiction outside of the United States makes this distinction.

As the immediate past chairman of the National Futures Association, the U.S. self-regulatory organization for futures markets, I sense there is a growing recognition within the Commodity Futures Trading Commission and Congress that regulatory reform is needed. The NFA, even without legislative action, has been able to reason with the CFTC in taking certain steps in the direction of two-tiered regulation, particularly in the area of managed money.

In 1997 the industry had an excellent opportunity to achieve congressional support for futures regulatory reform. However, the issue became confused with "pro markets" and the insistence in some quarters to drive home an agenda of two-tier markets. Momentum and support was lost, and the push for a legislative mandate for regulatory reform failed. I am optimistic enough to say that a renewed effort would succeed—but only if the agenda does not include pro markets.

Along the same line, how can retail traders cope with the clout of the funds?

Hansen: I'm not sure I understand the question. My firm did no retail business. Futures funds traders must enter the markets like all other participants, albeit in significant volumes. The retail traders are increasingly well-served by electronic order-entry Internet access through firms that specialize in handling retail business. Such traders may unwittingly step into the market just as "the funds" are going the other direction. Therefore, orders must be timed thoughtfully, at levels reflecting a careful trading plan. There is always a timing risk, but it is not a matter of fund clout versus a retail trader's goals.

Picking up on another theme you mentioned several times, how beneficial would common clearing be for institutional traders?

Hansen: The whole idea behind common clearing is to improve operating efficiencies, drive costs out of the system, and introduce savings through net margining and/or cross-margining opportunities. Apart from that, a combined clearing entity will present a stronger counterparty risk profile to institutional investors than is currently the case.

Allow me to explode a common myth about common clearing. Many in the industry, including a broad segment of CME and CBOT floor traders and brokers, have been led to believe that the aim of common clearing is to accomplish savings that, in turn, increase FCM profitability. This could not be further from the truth.

The fact is that any "systemic" savings are passed on quickly in the form of lower fees to market users—the customers. Competition among FCMs ensures this. Average institutional commission rates over the last 20 years have been driven down from the mid-$20 range to mid-single digits as FCMs were forced to pass on cost savings resulting from computerized back-office systems and other operating efficiencies. Exchange fees and floor brokerage, although declining, have been stubbornly defended and have not given up as much percentage-wise as FCM commission rates.

Thus, common clearing will soon result in lower transaction costs to all market users. This is critical to keeping U.S. futures markets competitive with the ever-expanding offshore exchanges and proliferating over-the-counter alternatives.

Your first "easy" prediction concerned the computerization of the industry. How will advances in technology, including electronic trading, affect the futures industry and traders in the next five years?

Hansen: Technology will rule every phase of the futures and derivatives trading agenda over the next five years and beyond.

Remember "PMS"? It was the indelicately named "Post Market System" and announced by CME Chairman Emeritus Leo Melamed at the September 1987 Swiss Commodity Futures and Options Association Conference in Burgenstock, Switzerland. Fortunately, the concept was redubbed "Globex" shortly thereafter. Thus, the seed of massive change in the futures industry was planted.

It was very slow to germinate and was met with huge emotional and political resistance every step of the way. For a time, the Luddites and self-serving interests prevailed.

But the momentum has clearly changed. In early 1998, for example, we witnessed the conquest of DTB (Deutsche Terminbörse) screen-trading on German bunds over the LIFFE open-outcry system. Both Chicago exchanges sense the threat, and their leaders are scrambling to get a strategy in place for a comprehensive technological response. The floor memberships are confused and fearful of the battle. And they are still generally in denial. This will all change, and "electronification" of the industry will develop very rapidly.

Another significant development that is occurring at the same time is the European Economic and Monetary Union. How will the new European currency affect the futures industry and traders?

Hansen: European Economic and Monetary Union has already had a dramatic effect on all aspects of the global futures industry. After several years of false starts and frustration—and facing considerable skepticism from the financial community—it is now clear that a single European currency will become a reality.

The most obvious impact of this on the futures industry is that several interest rate and currency contracts will cease to trade as 11 economies merge their monetary units into the Euro. Others will follow in the next few years.

All European exchanges, which have been the fastest growing engines of the global futures industry over the last decade, will have to adapt. Some will fail, others will merge, and all will undergo significant modifications.

The "shootout" between the DTB and LIFFE exchanges for European dominance and the struggle between open-outcry and screen-traded processes are the most graphic manifestations of the changes being wrought by monetary union. The astonishingly rapid "electronification" of Matif (Marché a Terme International de France) is another highly visible symptom of the immense changes all elements of the global futures industry must deal with going into the new millenium. "Adapt or die" is the unmistakable war cry.

Traders not only will have to learn new instruments, but they also will have to build skills in the new mediums in which they will be required to trade. FCMs will find it necessary to reinvent themselves entirely, including their processes for providing market access, clearing services, information management, and other customer services. The challenges to exchanges should be readily apparent. Even the regulators must rise to the need to respond quickly and effectively to this tidal wave of change.

Where will potential new users of futures and options get their education about trading in this new environment?

Hansen: The process of educating market users traditionally has been the purview of the exchanges and FCMs. In the case of "locals" or "market-makers," the clearing firms specializing in servicing that segment have performed that function.

The same "educators" will continue to carry this responsibility going forward but clearly in a much more diversified and creative way if they are to succeed. The Internet and other computerized processes will play a critical role and will offer educational and trading access to a much broader cross section of potential market participants.

It is also likely that this area will receive considerably more focus at the university undergraduate and business school level. Specialized training institutions may emerge. The age of real-time, real-money "financial trading games" is emerging and will be immensely popular.

Sorting through all these changes that you foresee, as well as your "easy" and difficult predictions for what lies ahead, what do you think is the single most important futures industry issue or development for traders in the next five years?

Hansen: I'm glad you asked. Allow me to give you the "Hansen Theory" of futures development over the next five years.

The single most important development can be characterized by two words—mergers and alliances. This is the only road to survival and success for this industry in the twenty-first century.

Common clearing among the CBOT, CME, and NYMEX must and will happen. The underlying logic is totally compelling. The politics are difficult, but it is only the beginning of what is to come—a practice run, if you will—for the real game. The real game—remember, you heard it here first—is that the Chicago Board of Trade and the Chicago Mercantile Exchange must merge.

The sooner this happens, the better for all constituencies, including member traders and floor brokers, futures commission merchants, proprietary traders, and member institutions and commercial firms. Furthermore, the professional staffs of a merged exchange will benefit through increased and long-term career opportunities.

Most of all, the market users of all dimensions and all conceivable interests will benefit. It is ironic that outside of Cook County, Illinois, even the most sophisticated market users make little distinction between the CME and the CBOT. To most participants, it is *Chicago* where they trade.

To do nothing, or to change too slowly, will be the kiss of death for the futures industry in Chicago. Everyone loses— members, customers, employees . . . indeed, the global economy. Inexorable forces are already in motion that will change everything. The challenge is huge, but so are the opportunities—if the right responses are made.

We are not talking open outcry versus electronic trading here. This has been an immense emotional issue in Chicago. To a great extent, it comes from the fears of the "traditional" members, the "full badge" holders in the grain and livestock markets who, in turn, have the most votes at both the CBOT and CME. Electronic trading doesn't "suit" their markets. "Physical" markets trade differently than interest rates, currencies, and equities, where cash and futures markets are totally fungible. Also, grain and livestock commercial users are not clamoring for computer trading like the financial sector, which already employs multiple electronic trading processes.

I agree with these arguments. But why do we refuse to recognize legitimate differences and insist on the "one size fits all" approach to exchange strategies?

Here are some of the steps I suggest:

- Merge the CBOT and the CME and clear on the common platform of a newly established Chicago Clearing Corporation.

- The merged Chicago exchanges—let's call it the Chicago International Futures Exchange (CIFEX) for now— reorganize as a new entity having four divisions, each with an operating committee responsible to a joint board of directors:

  Agricultural Division.   Grains and livestock and any new "physical" contracts would be grouped together on the same trading floor. The open-outcry trading process, which best accommodates the requirements of this contract class, will be preserved and enhanced through electronic order delivery and information management processes. A "traditional" way of life, for the most part, endures.

  Debt Instrument Division.   Global competition from the European and cash broker-sponsored exchanges will dictate that these markets convert to a computerized trading process. Otherwise, the franchise will be lost. A state-of-the-art system will be developed or adapted from an existing system.

  Currency Division.   As with debt instruments, the process will go totally electronic but in a form that preserves the value of a controlled, centralized trading program and mutual clearing. Advantages over interbank trading can be devised.

  Equity Products Division.   This sector is clearly a candidate for electronic trading and central clearing and should be designed hand in hand with the equities industry, accommodating customary existing practices such as block trading and crossing of trades. There will also be a huge retail and middle-institutional demand for these products, plus trading opportunities for "electronic locals."

- Current memberships are converted into common stock in the new entity on an equitable basis, reflecting relative values at the time of conversion. Include an initial public offering to extract value and market liquidity in the shares.

- A specified shareholding is required to obtain trading rights or permits in the various divisions or contract groupings.

- The new entity would be run as a profit-making organization yielding a dividend flow and increased share value for its stockholders. These are to be the primary objectives of a team of experienced, professional managers engaged to run the company. A well-rounded board of managers, shareholders, and outside directors would be constituted.

- Growth, innovation, flexibility, and competitiveness will be the driving forces to achieve corporate objectives, similar to other profit-oriented, global organizations.

- The four divisions will be managed according to their specific characteristics and requirements, within the general administration and policies of the corporation.

What will happen to local traders in this scenario? Are they a dying breed?

Hansen: Not at all. Arguably, this is the most exciting opportunity emerging from all the changes. Consider the concept of "electronic locals," which will preserve opportunities for those who have this special talent, who are risk-takers and who have adequate capitalization. This is where the most precious futures commodity of all—liquidity—can be preserved and nurtured. It also will solve the dilemma of what to do with all the trading floor real estate the exchanges have built in Chicago. Let me explain the vision.

When the computerization process in financial futures and options takes place as I have outlined, locals and order fillers in those markets will have very limited alternatives. The interaction and trading opportunities of open outcry will disappear.

Decisive and imaginative action on the part of the management of the newly formed CIFEX can convert this into a splendid opportunity by transforming the bond, Eurodollar, and currency floors into electronic trading arenas. This should be far more appealing to current and aspiring "locals" than the prospect of trading in isolation at home or "upstairs."

Rather, simple reengineering of these spaces, along with creatively programmed "electronic local" screens, can create an attractive trading ambiance, with opportunities not unlike today's trading floor environment.

Positioned comfortably in trading booths or stations in amphitheater style around the room, electronic locals will have at their fingertips state-of-the-art computer trading screens that show the depth and breadth of the market five tics on either side of the last trade. Customer screens will only see the last trade, bid, and offer on their direct-order screens. Only permit-holding shareowners will see what the locals and FCM order fillers see—much like the market is in open outcry. This "shareholder edge" is the price institutional and public participants should be willing to pay to ensure liquidity—the X factor that underlies the success and usefulness of the Chicago futures markets.

Electronic locals will be fed a constant stream of instant market information from large overhead screens in the middle of the floor. Quote boards on the perimeter walls, much like today, will give online recaps of all pertinent market activity. Traders will have the social and psychological stimuli of real colleagues to talk with to exchange ideas and sense the "pulse" of the markets.

Clearing firms will function much as they do today, sponsoring electronic locals, facilitating customer order-handling processes, clearing and accounting for their trades, exercising risk controls, and providing strategic information resources.

The combined processes as described allow each participant and firm to focus on what they do best, without all the political game-playing. The business will be driven by profit-motivated leadership, professional business managers who know that the only road to success is a competitive strategy that focuses on meeting customers' ever-changing requirements.

Ultimately, what is at stake here for the future of futures trading, especially in Chicago?

Hansen: The good news is that if customer-focused, user-friendly, reasonably regulated and liquid, centrally traded, and cleared markets are available, the world will clamor to participate. These instruments have proven their worth, and their potential has barely been tapped.

Of course, none of this will take place in isolation. Eurex (formerly DTB and Swiss Options and Financial Futures Exchange), LIFFE, Tokyo International Financial Futures Exchange, Cantor Fitzgerald, Prebon Yamane, and all the other existing and "wannabe" exchanges are plotting their own survival and success strategies. We will be surprised by their innovation and aggressiveness. They must be watched very closely. We have a lot to learn from them. Counterdefensive measures must be employed.

Clearly, the time is at hand to make dramatic changes that can restore Chicago to its rightful place as the leader of global derivatives trading. The potential for growth in this new environment is enormous. The opportunity must not be squandered because of shortsightedness or political self-indulgence. There will not be a second chance.

STRIVING FOR EFFICIENCY

Yra G. Harris
President
Praxis Trading and Arbitrage

Yra Harris has been actively involved in the futures industry for a number of years as a manager of operations for several brokerage firms, as a commodity trading advisor, and as a member of the board of directors of the Chicago Mercantile Exchange (CME). He is a registered CTA, floor broker, and commodity pool operator.

Harris has been a partner of Praxis Trading and Arbitrage since 1979. He began his career in the industry as a manager and floor trader for B. International Foreign Currency Arbitrage from 1977 to 1979 and served as an independent order filler for James Sinclair & Co., a major New York-based currency and gold trading firm, from 1979 to 1983. He became a commodity trading advisor for Harris-Furman Commodity Trading Advisory Co. from 1987 to 1989 and a partner of Jet Blast Inc. (Chicago Mercantile Exchange), 1989 to 1990, prior to his affiliation with Gandalf Asset Management Corporation.

As a member of the CME, he has served three terms as the elected chairman of the International Monetary Market Nomi-

nating Committee and has been a member of a number of com-
mittees and task forces, including Currency Task Force Review
Group, Business Conduct, Computer Trade Reconstruction,
Dual Trading, Financial Instruments Steering, Exchange for
Physicals, Floor Practices, Globex Screen Design, and Mem-
bership. He is also a member of the Commodity Futures
Trading Commission (CFTC) Financial Instruments Steering
Committee.

**You are known for your expertise in matters related to
technology and foreign currency trading, so let's start
with the technology theme, which has affected all areas
of our lives. How do you think technology will affect exchanges, brokerage firms, and traders the most in the
next few years?**

Harris: There is a lot of talk about electronic trading, but I view
technology as being most valuable for its ability to speed the
process of order entry and exit from the pits. I believe the
open-outcry, auction-type market is the best mechanism for
price discovery and for creating price transparency. One of the
problems with electronic systems is that when you need them
the most, they tend to be the most inefficient, as several examples attest.

The value of technology really enters into the system in its
ability to expedite order entry and order exit. It will enhance the
delivery of orders to the order filler in a very fast and efficient
way and will send them back to the clearing firm and the ultimate customer in a very fast and expedient manner. Those who
learn how to use this technology will become even more efficient at doing what they do, which will lead to greater incomes
down the road than they are receiving now because I think their
order flow will increase.

If we are successful at improving order processing, open outcry will have a long life ahead of it because I believe it is the best
method for bringing buyers and sellers together.

Then what about the electronic trading systems that seem to be gaining momentum? What are the downsides of this technology?

Harris: The pit operates better in active market conditions, which I would say would be 20 or 25 percent of the time. The problem with electronic matching systems—the interbank market is full of this—is that people who are good market-makers are not able to find much of a profit margin. Traders aren't free. I trade markets all over the world, and I certainly expect to pay the professional for being there to make a market. If you stop paying professionals to be there to make a market, they naturally will stop being there. Then, when you really need them, they are not going to be there and you are going to wonder, "What have I done?"

I think this is what the banks are doing in some markets. They are squishing a lot of traders out of the game, and only a handful of major market-makers will be left. If you think that's to the advantage of people searching for prices, you are highly mistaken. It's like anything else: When you squish out all the competitors, you have a free hand and can widen out those margins.

There is more to the market than just price. So much of the market is about gathering information and trading information with other people to see what they know. The price is determined by what information you gather and the conclusions you make from it. Trading screens don't gather information. People do. The person who is able to analyze and disseminate information will become even more valuable. People will be sucked into the trap of pure electronics, but the markets need more than that. That's why I think the future of exchanges is great—nowhere else can you find that kind of pricing mechanism.

How will technology affect jobs at the exchanges or in the futures industry?

Harris: I think people get depressed when they think about any major changes. The history of any technological change from the 1700s on is about people who are upset about what is coming—the Luddites in England in the 1840s, everybody who worked in a buggy factory in Detroit in the early 1900s. . . . But technology has a way of displacing and dislocating jobs and then recreating them in another fashion. The smart people who understand how to utilize the technology they're given and adapt themselves will always come out okay.

Will there be a lot of clerk jobs that will disappear if technology is sufficient? Yes. Will they all disappear? Certainly not. I don't know what the number will be; the market will create that. We'll have to figure out how best to use this technology to make the markets more efficient.

A number of people I interviewed for this book, like myself, started their careers as runners and clerks on the exchange floor. If the role of the clerk is diminishing, where are the best opportunities today for starting a career in the industry?

Harris: That's an interesting question because I recently had the pleasure of addressing a class of graduate students in international economics and finance at Brandeis University. They are very astute when it comes to these things. A lot of them are going to establish themselves as traders from scratch. Their computer expertise is far beyond what most people here on the floor have today. They know how to avail themselves of technology.

They will create mega opportunities, as some of the younger people on the floor in the Eurodollar pit are doing, for example. Although some people are crying that there's no business, they are setting up elaborate operations and have been tremendously successful. There will always be opportunities—huge opportunities—in the emerging markets. Capital is floating around the world in phenomenal amounts, growing all the time. I think the opportunities are endless; you just have to adapt to what the situations are.

Look at the big picture and see how much money has gone into the stock market—everybody I know who doesn't know a thing about finances has been making more money in the market than they ever dreamed of. That is going to end. I don't know when it's going to end, but when it does, a big group of people are no longer going to be happy with returns of 8 or 10 percent, which used to be phenomenal. People have become wedded to the idea of 25 or 30 percent returns for a couple of years. That makes our industry that much more viable because if you go back over the last 30 or 40 years, the only place you could have that kind of return was in futures.

And once the stock market turns down . . .?

Harris: It doesn't even have to turn down, I don't think. It just stops performing. If the stock market breaks 20 or 25 percent and sits there for the next three years, people are going to be beside themselves trying to generate returns like they've gotten in recent years. And where are they going to find them? At that point, they are still in the greed stage. Eventually they will get to the other stage, fear, but investors haven't even thought about protecting capital yet. So there could be quite a window of opportunity for futures for some time.

You mentioned the opportunities in emerging markets. The CME is now trading the Russian ruble, and that area of the world has been in economic turmoil. What trading opportunities do you see involving Russia and Eastern Europe overall?

Harris: So many things are possible there that we can't even comprehend what the outcome will be at this time. Eastern Europe is going to take many twists and turns, which is certainly what the trader searches for. Certainly Eastern Europe is attractive as you look at what the Germans are doing. Everybody talks about the European Economic and Monetary Union (EMU) and Western Europe, but German investment goes into Eastern and Central Europe and is not directed to

Western Europe. They see unexploited opportunities—great untapped potential.

And Russia? Who knows about Russia? Russia is still trying to develop its capital markets and has unbelievable potential. They are trying to develop a stock market and a bond market, and they don't want to depend on short-term capital flows to finance their development. That was a mistake made by a lot of countries in Asia that were so dependent on "hot money," which creates crisis when it leaves. I think the Russians are trying to establish a sound financial system, but there is still a question whether they can get it done.

The European currency changes obviously have major ramifications for currency trading at the CME. How will that affect the exchange and traders over time?

Harris: We view it as a great opportunity because the only currency we trade that is really affected is the D-mark. We'll lose the French franc, too, of course, but that's not one of our most vibrant contracts on a day-to-day basis. We think the Euro will be a much more dynamic currency than the D-mark because it will be a much higher-weighted reserve currency with a much broader base of circulation and greater volatility. From a trader's perspective, I think we are looking at a vast expansion in currency trading. This is a very good move for us, requiring very little adjustment.

Currencies are traded around the clock and more markets are getting that way. How will technicians determine what a trading "day" is and where will they get their data?

Harris: Well, you always have Globex charts. A lot of traders who only had International Monetary Market charts now keep 24-hour charts based on the pricing mechanism on Globex because that market has become so efficient. You just keep charts all day, using the technology that is now available and adjusting to it. I have been keeping 24-hour cash charts for currencies for 10 years, so it's no big change. It is a 24-hour market, so you deal with it on that basis if you want to trade it.

Years ago we had to fight with the CFTC to allow 24-hour access to our markets via EFPs (exchange for physicals), which were needed then. They are not even needed any more because we have the facilities, via Globex, to do all kinds of size whenever you want except for a couple of minutes every day. It is seamless, and you can do any business you want in a regulated market. The problem with the EFP market is that, because it's off exchange, it's an unregulated pricing mechanism and customers really don't know if they're attaining the best price at the time they need to make a deal.

A lot of firms like to capture the EFP business and make money on making the market and then move it to the exchanges where they can also collect a commission. So this has been an area of conflict. Regulators need to be aware that with our electronic mechanism—not just Globex but Project A at the Chicago Board of Trade and others—you don't need these other vehicles because you can bring them to a centralized marketplace with a much more transparent mechanism.

One of the big problems that exists today is the unregulated nature of the derivatives market. Nobody is looking over that game. I am not in favor of rampant regulation, but some regulation is needed in that area, especially in the over-the-counter market. It is amazing to me that nearly every major disaster has happened in the back room of banks. You have a $30 trillion evaluation in the derivatives market—unregulated. The room for systemic risk is great.

With your knowledge of technology, you probably are involved in the Year 2000 question. What's your take on that whole issue and what it means for traders?

Harris: I'm not smart enough to tell you whether this issue is being overblown or not. The exchanges have spent a lot of money to make sure their computers are ready, and in fact, we have spent money trying to help our clearing firms. We're preparing for it, but beyond that I don't know.

One of the biggest plays of the year has been some trader who put on a huge "millenium butterfly." He bought September 1999 Euros, sold December 1999, and bought March 2000 because he thought the borrowing cost to meet this issue would be greatest in that time frame. It was a big hit; he made a lot of money on it. That shows how traders capitalize on such situations and turn them into trading opportunities.

Europe, of course, has a bigger problem because they have to get their computers to switch over to Euro denominations at the same time. Their costs are enormous.

You hear so much talk about Year 2000, but I don't know what will happen. As usual, one of the good things about markets is that, if you give them a little chance to make a profit, someone will find a solution.

What's your view about another recent issue, the two-tier marketplace?

Harris: I have problems with that. Does that mean because I'm a little guy, I'm getting screwed? Does a big guy get a better price? The great thing about exchanges is that they don't care whether you are big or little. If you do have to move huge size, we have a facility at the CME for that, all-or-none pricing, which means the customer gets a price for all of the contracts or none. It can violate an immediate price, but the price by which it is violated is so minimal that usually somebody will take you out anyway and facilitate your trade.

I know the CFTC has talked about this for the professional. But I think you are really walking in dangerous territory. The little guy should not have the short end of the stick. It's like taking somebody who knows how to trade foreign exchange and another person who has to get foreign exchange at an airport vending booth, where he or she can get destroyed. Now, is that what you want to encourage? I don't. I want all customers to feel they are as much a part of the system as everyone else is.

What about common clearing? How important is that for the exchanges and traders?

Harris: I know the good sides, I know the efficiencies that are developed, but I think the final word on that issue still has to be determined by our membership. They have to view it as what are we getting in value versus what are we giving up. In the present proposal the exchange is being asked to give up one of its jewels, our clearing mechanism. I think this might happen eventually and will lead to greater economies of scale, but it is going to be an arduous fight.

I am in favor of everything that creates efficiencies because I think we have tolerated some inefficiencies in this business for too long. We are no different than any other business in this world—you have to be as efficient as your competition or you will die.

What about a total merger of the Chicago exchanges?

Harris: You never know. I think it's still a dream. But when people dream, funny things happen. Of course, it may be a nightmare.

What is the single most important issue or development for individual traders in the next 5 to 10 years?

Harris: Their ability to access the markets in a fast way—fast in and fast out. That's what Schwab and others are offering equities traders, and that's what we as an exchange have to correct to bring traders all the way into the pit. The idea of keeping the trader—commodity trading advisor, bank, what have you—out of the pit is going to fall by the wayside.

Your exchange membership is going to give you a commission advantage and the ability to be right there to trade the flow, but you are not going to be able to keep customers out of the pit. You have to provide them some type of access. That will be the technological advance we need to accomplish.

VIEW FROM DOWN UNDER

Leslie V. Hosking
Chief Executive Officer and Director
Sydney Futures Exchange

Les Hosking has been involved in the futures industry for most of his working life, beginning his career in 1966 as a wool futures trader for J.W. McGregor, a founding floor member of the Sydney Greasy Wool Futures Exchange. In 1969 he began a 10-year association with the Japanese multinational firm Itochu as a futures trader and client advisor and from 1974 as manager of the Itochu futures operations in Australia.

In 1979 Hosking was appointed divisional manager of clearing services at International Commodities Clearing House (ICCH), Australia, which was the clearinghouse for the Sydney Futures Exchange (SFE). In 1984 he was based in Singapore and Kuala Lumpur as ICCH's regional representative in Asia.

Hosking assumed his current position as chief executive officer and director of the Sydney Futures Exchange on January 2, 1985. He also is a director of SFE's two wholly owned subsidiaries, Sydney Futures Exchange Clearing House and New Zealand Futures & Options Exchange. During his tenure, SFE has been ranked as the largest financial futures exchange in the Asia-Pacific zone ahead of equivalent exchanges in Tokyo,

Singapore, and Hong Kong, and it is now the eleventh largest futures exchange in the world.

Hosking has been appointed to a number of boards and committees, including the Australian government's newly formed Financial Sector Advisory Council, which will play a vital role in advising the government on policies that will ensure that Australia develops as an efficient, competitive, and dynamic financial sector.

As one of the open-outcry exchanges at the center of the electronic trading debate, the Sydney Futures Exchange made the decision to go electronic and away from the trading floor. What is the plan for that to happen?

Hosking: SFE is scheduled to introduce in December 1998 its new Windows NT 4.0 version of SYCOM®, including open architecture designed to interface with most automated order-entry interfaces. The actual closure of the floor will then depend upon the speed at which the SFE members convert fully to the electronic platform. Based on the Matif (Marché a Terme International de France) example, there may not be a long transition time.

In any event, SFE intends to list a number of products full time on SYCOM IV from January 1999 with capacity for interfaces to Sydney from London, Chicago, New York, and other major financial centers.

Looking beyond the SFE for the moment and at the futures and options industry in general, what do you view as the key factors that will determine how trades will be executed as we move into the next century?

Hosking: Immediacy and liquidity will continue to influence how trades are executed. However, in the future electronic markets will ultimately prove to be able to provide immediate liquid markets at a lower cost than open-outcry floors.

You mentioned the Matif example. What lesson did that provide the industry?

Hosking: The sudden transition by Matif from open outcry to the screen is the forerunner of how other open-outcry markets may make the transition. Matif decided on a strategy of operating the floor and screen simultaneously to allow its participants to make their own choice. The rapid move by the brokers and institutions to screens, leaving the locals on the floor to trade with themselves, gives other exchanges a model of how to depoliticize the issue of floor versus screen.

What about other electronic alternatives such as the Cantor Fitzgerald proposal?

Hosking: The Cantor Fitzgerald proposal is living proof that electronic alternatives to open-outcry floors can be formed. Taken in the context of how quickly the institutions in Matif moved to electronic trading when given the choice, why would the same not happen in U.S. markets or generally between exchange-traded markets and over-the-counter (OTC) markets?

How will all of these developments affect the institutional trader? The retail trader?

Hosking: Electronic trading will eliminate many profit opportunities between the "bid" and "ask" that are available to individual traders in the open-outcry pits. Consequently, there will be more institution-to-institution execution and less intermediation.

In liquid markets where the spread will remain narrow, there will be less fragmentation of institutional traders. In less liquid markets the spreads will be wider; however, matching algorithms will be developed to overcome this problem. Ultimately, the computer algorithm will be the substitute intermediary for both retail and institutional traders.

What is the outlook for international exchange links, and how will this affect traders?

Hosking: Major FCMs and investment banks already have access to all the exchanges that they deem necessary to trade on and, in many cases, can already electronically deliver their business to those exchanges. With the further development of both electronic order-entry software and open-architecture interfaces at electronic exchanges, linkages between exchanges are becoming unnecessary for FCMs and investment banks.

How will the Sydney Futures Exchange preserve the role of the retail broker and trader?

Hosking: Retail brokers on the SFE will continue to control the gateway into the exchange for customer business. Retail brokers will continue to provide traditional services to customers beyond execution. It is our experience to date in electronic trading that most customers continue to use brokers primarily to avoid the risks associated with execution and the infrastructure and regulatory costs associated with having full-time direct access.

One of the overriding themes in all of business in the 1990s has been the advance of technology. In addition to the electronic trading issue, how will this trend affect the futures industry and individual traders in the next five years?

Hosking: Technology will significantly alter the futures industry in the near term. The differentiation between exchange-traded markets and over-the-counter markets will be diminished, if not eliminated. Cash and derivatives markets will be presented to institutions and retail traders side-by-side onscreen. This is what the institutions want as part of cost rationalization.

The "new breed" of individual traders should find technology of significant benefit by way of better live information and tools to analyze the information and execute the trades rapidly. Technology will also widen the scope of markets that individual traders can access simultaneously.

How will the new European currency affect the futures industry and individual traders?

Hosking: The Euro will reduce the multiple-market opportunities currently available in Europe, which will be of benefit to the Asia-Pacific markets in attracting added business.

What other markets are most vulnerable to change in the next 5 to 10 years?

Hosking: The trading floor of the New York Stock Exchange (NYSE).

Why do you think the NYSE floor will be threatened?

Hosking: NYSE faces competitive challenges from Nasdaq domestically and the single European market, including the London Stock Exchange/Deutsche Terminbörse alliance, internationally. Both of these marketplaces are expanding aggressively and improving access and price discovery via electronic technology.

NYSE continues to be committed to its floor and specialist system in the face of growing evidence that the fully electronic, nonspecialist markets are more cost-effective but equal in liquidity.

What do you see as the single most important futures industry issue or development in the next five years?

Hosking: Online clearing.

How will exchange services change in an era of more round-the-clock trading where there is no end or no beginning to the "trading day"? Who will provide the data traders need?

Hosking: To facilitate traders who require an end-of-day or start-day price, SFE is developing an electronic matching program that can be operated at a nominated point in the day—the start or the end of the day. The program is similar to an old-fashioned opening call on the trading floors of the 1950s where an opening or closing price level is determined according to the maximum quantities that can be executed at that time at the best equitable price.

What is your opinion about a two-tier market with two sets of regulations, one for retail traders and one for institutional traders? Would this benefit retail traders?

Hosking: Retail traders are already more than adequately regulated because the regulating agencies have been styled to regulate the retail end. It will benefit the industry if institutional trading is regulated on an equivalent basis to the less-regulated OTC markets.

THE RETAIL VOICE

Barry J. Lind
Chairman
Lind-Waldock & Co.

As the founder and chairman of a major brokerage firm and as a board member of the Chicago Mercantile Exchange (CME), Barry J. Lind has been one of the most active leaders in the futures industry over the last 30 years.

He began trading in 1962 and within three years had developed enough public business to open his own firm, Lind-Waldock & Co., which is now the largest discount brokerage firm in the futures industry and one of the leading proponents in developing and using technology. His firm was among the earliest to automate its order-routing system and to offer on-line trading.

In 1970 Lind was elected to the first of five terms on the CME Board of Governors. He was instrumental in creating the CME's International Monetary Market (IMM) and served as its vice chairman. He has been a member of the most influential CME committees, including Strategic Planning, Common Goals, Financial Instruments, Membership Expansion, International Steering, and a number of others.

Lind was instrumental in developing the exchange's Computer Trade Reconstruction (CTR) program and continues to serve on the CTR committee. He was a major advocate in introducing the S&P 500 Index E-mini contract, the first product to be traded electronically during the CME's regular business hours.

Lind's leadership role within the futures industry includes serving on the National Futures Association (NFA) board of directors for 12 years and on the NFA's finance committee. He also is a member of the Financial Products Advisory Committee, one of a select number of advisory committees to the Commodity Futures Trading Commission, and the Futures Industry Association's Task Force to Promote Common Clearing.

Lind is also the author of *Method Trading,* first published in 1969 and since translated into seven languages with more than 100,000 copies in circulation.

With your background, you are in an excellent position to speak on issues related to the impact of technology on exchanges, brokerage firms, and traders—virtually every facet of the futures industry. How do you think the advance of technology will affect brokerage firms such as yours in the next five years?

Lind: The advance of technology will affect brokerage firms in several ways. On the plus side, technology means that processes can be automated, and management can do more systematic and thorough analysis of risks, costs, and market opportunities. It also means that brokerage firms, in the process of discovering how their clients use their services, will have the potential to customize services and target exactly those clients who will find them attractive. The ability will exist to micromarket to niche audiences and to deliver a wide range of information in an inexpensive way.

On the other hand, the costs associated with technology development and maintenance are steep. And the development of technology, with its ability to offer services such as online trading, is leading brokerage firms to do some soul-searching about what kind of value they bring to certain transactional processes. Fees charged for some traditional services will need to be restructured to reflect their value to the client.

How about this client? Your firm probably has more experience with more smaller, retail traders than any other firm today. How will this trader be affected by technology?

Lind: Retail customers will certainly be able to exercise more control over their financial decisions, whether it's trading, getting research, moving money between accounts, or any one of a variety of functions brokerages may offer. But there's too much competition right now for the customers' investment dollars—or whatever currency they use.

Eventually, customers will enter their own orders. Commissions will come down. But at that point, there will be a dramatic increase in the number of investors who come to the futures markets to trade because the markets will be much more attractive and accessible.

How will order routing and trade execution take place as we move into the next century?

Lind: Firms have already automated big parts of the order-routing process. It was clear long ago that any business that handled as many transactions and accounts as we did for execution, clearing, and settlement had to automate significant parts of its operation. It's been almost 15 years since I sat down with my information technology staff and designed "Order Express," the backbone of Lind-Waldock's system.

The two newest developments that have had the most impact on the order-routing and execution processes are on the front end—that is, technology is now in the hands of the end user through the extension of inexpensive networks like the Internet, and on the execution end, orders are being carried to electronic systems that match trades and send back executions.

Trading systems at exchanges that are fully electronic have been around for a long time, but futures traders in the United States had never been exposed to any product in electronic form in which they had much interest until the Chicago Mercantile

Exchange offered its S&P 500 Index E-mini electronically during the exchange's regular daytime trading hours.

What role will the Internet play in this process?

Lind: I think Internet order routing will win out with investors who are technology literate and who are comfortable directing their own trading. This group gets larger every day. There are generational differences—I'll probably never be as comfortable with computers as my daughter is, but I'm getting better and so are my cohorts. As technology becomes even more pervasive and user friendly, the differences will become less distinct.

And it's not simply a comfort with technology. It's the ability of investors to find information about events and markets and to manipulate increasingly available market data that gives confidence to futures traders.

There will always be investors who don't want to take investing into their own hands so much, and brokers will need to accommodate them. That most likely means that someone at a brokerage firm will enter the order into an electronic order-routing system because the order will either be going to an electronic system or to a trading floor that's hooked seamlessly into electronic order-routing systems. If the trading floors are to survive in anything that looks like their current form, the only way it can happen is with electronic interfaces all the way up to the point of execution.

So what do you expect technology to do to the traditional trading floor in the debate between open outcry and electronic trading?

Lind: Most of the battles between open outcry and electronic systems generate more heat than light. As long as investors can be assured they are getting speed and certainty in the execution process and as long as I can take advantage of the efficiencies of automation all the way up to the point of execution, I'm less interested in whether the order is executed on an electronic system or on a trading floor. At that point, the market can decide whether the advantages in liquidity generation that are supposed to exist in an open-outcry, competitive environment justify the overhead involved in maintaining the system.

And the argument over the comparative advantages of the electronic systems that the exchanges are developing will resolve itself because I think eventually all the systems will offer pretty much the same features. They'll all mimic the most desirable features of each one. At that point, maybe a standard platform and systems interfaces will be possible.

The bottom line is that open outcry can live if it gets faster. Right now it's too slow. You put in a buy order and you don't know whether you're filled or not. You could have a really big profit, but by the time you find out about your fill, the market's on the way down. So the big profit is gone. Maybe you find out about your fill fast enough to take a little profit or maybe no profit or maybe even a loss. This kind of stuff has to go away.

In this environment, what will be the role of the "traditional" broker and floor trader in the years ahead?

Lind: Again, the changes that have happened just since the beginning of 1998 are startling. Matif (Marché a Terme International de France), the French futures exchange that had copied the open-outcry system, abandoned its trading floor to go completely electronic, even though it had decided initially to offer side-by-side open outcry and electronic trading. Why? The business quickly migrated to the electronic system, and trading volume doubled in some products being traded only on the electronic platform. Sydney is closing its futures floor. The volume in the overnight electronic systems of the Chicago futures exchanges is picking up steadily, and the E-mini S&P contract that is traded electronically is doing well.

If the trading floors survive, it will be more necessary than ever for floor traders to be liquidity providers to earn their keep. And the "traditional" floor broker will be wired. In a floor or an electronic environment, there will always be some value added that brokers can offer in filling big orders by using the information flow available to them.

I think it's possible that floor trading may survive in some products but not in others. I've always thought that the agricultural markets are more resistant to being put on a screen, but I've always gotten dissenters who point to the Tokyo grain markets that are fully electronic. I told one of the exchange staff members 10 years ago that the exchanges started with the ag markets and would end up with the ag markets. I'm not so sure that I was right—at least with respect to floor trading at the exchanges. Either way, the traditional broker will always be able to fill orders in beans and cattle because I'm not sure who else would want those contracts.

How will the Internet affect how your customers get market information, data, etc.?

Lind: The Internet is an inexpensive network. There are an estimated 62 million people over the age of 18 online, and these people are developing the habit of going online to perform a growing range of functions. You can do tours of real estate online, you can calculate costs of refinancing your mortgage online, you can find out almost anything online. And customers will go online to get market data and information, either from their brokerage firms or from a whole variety of boutique providers who spring up to offer some specialized service.

The Internet has revolutionized the way people are accessing information. The brokerage business can't isolate itself from these trends. Not only will we use the Internet to send the standard kind of information that used to go by mail—account statements, confirmations, etc.—but we'll also be able to use the Internet to customize information for customers. We can match customers with information about services that we think they'll want to use and deliver the information at the time they're most likely to be thinking about using them. It's very targeted marketing, and it's where the world is going.

Sometimes the Internet is a mixed blessing: There are a wide range of problems with speed, security, and reliability, but ways are being developed to handle these complaints.

One of the factors in getting information and data—in fact, in the logistics of trading in general—is the matter of global trading. How will traders and brokerage firms deal with round-the-clock trading that has no end or beginning to the trading "day"?

Lind: Brokerage firms have to pick some end-of-day point for processing. But the risk management issues that arise when you're doing business across time zones will force us to take snapshots of positions and to do interim calculations, probably at least three times in a 24-hour period, at the end of the trading day in the Asian, European, and North American time zones. Traders will need to be on real-time systems, and the middle office function that tracks risk and positions for them will become more important.

Retail traders, by and large, stick to local markets that are open during normal business hours in their own time zone. Those are the markets that make the headlines in their newspapers and on their televisions. Those are the markets that most affect their lives. Retail traders in the United States will most often trade U.S. stock indexes, U.S. interest rates, or U.S. agricultural markets. Those markets are most liquid during U.S. business hours.

But events outside of normal business hours in a local time zone can have an effect on positions. And bigger trading windows mean that retail traders can enter protective stop orders that are executed before or after daytime hours or that they can enter a position in advance of the opening or after the close of the primary market.

The market participants that can trade most effectively in a variety of markets at any time of the day are funds.

How can the retail trader cope with the clout of the funds?

Lind: The so-called clout of the funds that you suggest is a function of their large size. The funds often put the markets out of sync because of the impact they have when they put on or take off positions. Retail traders can take advantage of the temporary distortions caused by the funds to better enter or exit their own positions. Because of this, it's wrong to believe that retail traders always get hurt by the large funds in the market.

Besides, the major difference between retail traders and the funds is staying power. A well-capitalized smaller trader shouldn't be bothered by the movement of funds into and out of the market if the trader has the right market insight and can afford to stay with it.

What about a two-tier market and two sets of regulations in the United States, one for individual traders and one for institutional traders? Would this benefit retail traders?

Lind: I have to look at this from the point of view of my retail customer. I've been serving these customers for 30 years, so I think I can speak to what they would want. My customers deserve protection, but a double set of regulations should not be used to keep a retail account from the benefits of participating in a market to which institutional traders have access.

An example is the currency market. Our customers would often be better off participating in the interbank market because it offers more choices of currencies, and many times it offers more liquidity. I don't believe my customers should be "protected" from the ability to access that liquidity and make those choices.

What about the stock index area? Why and how should the retail trader trade the newer, smaller index con-

tracts? And why should they trade these index futures instead of options?

Lind: The dollar value of older stock index contracts grew to stratospheric levels, with margin levels equally stratospheric. The new stock indexes are more affordable for individual investors and, because they are more affordable, give investors the ability to trade multiple contracts and to use more strategies. The smaller contracts have also been remarkably liquid for this early stage of their development.

Stock indexes give individuals the ability to protect their portfolio or to maximize their purchasing power. They're incredibly efficient instruments compared to buying or selling a comparable amount of stock, and they immediately reflect the entirety of the market's move. They can be used instead of options or with options. We recommend protective stop orders for our customers who trade stock indexes, as we do with any market that is volatile.

Other than the continuing challenge of the markets' ups and downs, what do you see as the single most important futures industry issue or development for individual traders in the next five years?

Lind: Without a doubt, the dominant issue will be the development of technology. That issue will not only be the most important for individual traders but also for the industry as a whole for all of the reasons we talked about before: order routing, trade execution, information delivery, risk management, operations management. It's hard to overestimate how important it is.

THE INSTITUTIONAL PERSPECTIVE

Laurence E. Mollner
President
Mariah Investment Company

Larry Mollner has more than 30 years of experience in the futures industry, primarily with Dean Witter Reynolds Inc. (DWR), and is currently president of Mariah Investment Company. He served as president of Carr Futures from August 1997 through January 31, 1998, after being responsible for the sale and transition of the Institutional Futures Division of DWR to Carr.

Mollner joined DWR in May 1979 as vice president of commercial sales of the Commodity Division. He went on to develop the Commodity Division's financial futures area, becoming first vice president and, in 1983, senior vice president. In 1985, he was named executive vice president and director of the Futures Markets Division of DWR.

He also was a member of the board of directors of Dean Witter International Ltd. in London and a board member of Demeter Management Corporation, a wholly owned subsidiary of DWR that acts as general partner to the DWR public futures funds.

Mollner has also been a prominent leader in the futures industry. He is the former chairman of the Futures Industry Association (FIA) and is currently a member of the board of directors as well as the FIA executive committee. He also is on the board of directors of the National Futures Association (NFA).

At the Chicago Mercantile Exchange (CME), Mollner serves as an industry governor, chairing or participating in numerous committees at the exchange.

You have had a broad range of experience in the futures industry, building an institutional brokerage business and being actively involved with the CME, FIA, and NFA. Let's begin with your overview of your segment of the futures industry and where it stands at this point.

Mollner: One cannot address institutional futures trading without exploring the shifting elements of the business, both retail and institutional. Over recent history—say, the last 25 years—there has been a shift in percentage makeup of market participants. The balance between floor traders (locals) and commercial (hedge) and speculative (retail) participants has moved to a much higher percentage of commercial activity. This general statement comes from the higher volumes traded in the financial futures markets, which did not start to come into existence until 1972.

I will also contend there has been a significant change on the brokerage side of the business. For example, prior to the boom in financial futures, most brokerage firms were full-service and offered futures trading along with equities. Although generally requiring a specialist, the firms trained or hired these futures specialists and provided a wide range of services including research, both fundamental and technical. With the lowering of commission rates due to competition, services provided by the large brokerage firms generally were reduced.

This was all coming about while institutional participation was growing. It wasn't hard to see that it took the same amount of time to execute and process the speculator's 1- or 5-lot order as it did for the 100- or 500-lot institutional order. In addition, the small speculative accounts were viewed as more of a compliance problem; smaller dollars were at risk, but they were a greater credit risk or collection problem.

Some will argue there has been little to no growth in retail participation but that it has merely shifted from the larger full-service brokerage firms to the smaller local introducing broker and the growing number of discount brokers.

What about the future for this business?

Mollner: Looking ahead, I see the obvious consolidation in the financial services industry taking both traders and brokers away from the markets, many financial firms being both. The speculator will always trade the market that is volatile, and I see no end to the basic laws of supply and demand on all products. I will even go so far as to say I don't believe economic cycles are dead either—which means if we have a period of high inflation and rising interest rates, we will see explosions in volumes, not only from the hedgers but also from speculators.

I also believe that with the ease of access to markets via the computer and Internet, some individuals who are now trading equities in the quiet of their home, doing their own research, etc., will drift over to futures speculation, particularly when we get a bear market in equities. The benefactors will be the discount brokerage firms and the speculators themselves.

It is important to also mention the growth of the commodity pool or fund business. Although managed accounts (professional traders handling other people's money under a power of attorney) have been around for decades, the real growth in the business came in the 1980s with the formation of limited partnerships and then the introduction of guaranty funds. This acceptance helped legitimize futures trading because it was marketed as an alternative asset class. It is estimated that some $25 to $28 billion is currently under management.

This, of course, adds another class of speculator to the makeup of the market—the professional traders. Most of these are systems traders (using computers to generate buy and sell signals). Their presence has changed the makeup of the market in that the large pool operator has to trade large size to manage portfolios effectively.

You mentioned computers and technology several times. How do you see changes in technology affecting the futures industry?

Mollner: For the professional trader, it provides almost unlimited methods of analyzing markets. With the speed of the computer and the advances in programming, we are finding many new ways to trade and, more important, over shorter time parameters.

As I mentioned, I also believe the individual private speculator will find that futures trading is not as scary as the stories would have you believe. You only have to understand leverage and apply the necessary disciplines of trading. With more and more individuals investing from home via the Internet, I think you will find a certain percentage will drift over to trade futures and options (both equity and futures). What would happen if only 2 percent of the individual equity traders started to trade futures?

On the institutional level, computer technology is improving the risk management systems for the institutional user of the market. Along with risk management comes the ability to analyze the markets more thoroughly. To improve on both the risk management and analytical sides, immediate impute of positions is essential. Management will require the trader to impute trades immediately, and the trader will demand that to be the same as the execution—in other words, single straight-through processing of orders will become the norm.

If my last scenario holds true, institutional traders themselves will demand screen-based trading systems. Currently, financial institutions that use both screen-based and open-outcry markets are seeing the benefits of trading via a screen.

I still believe that today open outcry is a faster method of trading in large markets like T-bonds and Eurodollars, but it is also a more costly method of trading. It is people-intensive and, therefore, also subject to delays and human error. You only have to look at the percentage of out-trades the next day to realize that the exposures in the marketplace are too high. The futures industry does a great job of clearing up its out-trades, but it is still a slower and more error-prone system when compared to a screen-based system.

Your comment makes it sound like open outcry is dead. How much time do you see before your scenario takes place, and what will happen to the markets as we know them today?

Mollner: Well, Scott, it's really hard to say. A few years ago I thought it would be 10 to 20 years. In reviewing some comments I made last year, I said 5 to 10 years. I now believe it is only 3 to 5 years.

The ability of some of the open-outcry exchanges like the Sydney Futures Exchange and Matif (Marché a Terme International de France) and possibly even LIFFE (London International Financial Futures Exchange) to make the dramatic switch to screens tells me it will come faster than we believe. The real question is not when will the markets switch to screens but will it happen with the current exchanges or will it happen some other way?

Let me give you a couple of scenarios. The three big U.S. futures exchanges—the Chicago Board of Trade, Chicago Mercantile Exchange, and New York Mercantile Exchange—are all member organizations, for the most part controlled by the floor population. They have a strong resistance to change, particularly when it comes to technological innovation. Therefore, it is quite possible the resistance will be so strong that the elected leadership of the exchanges will not be able to make the necessary changes fast enough for these institutions to survive. New entrants will be set up and approved by the regulators, and before the threatened exchanges realize it, they will have lost their market.

My preferred scenario would be one that has the current exchanges being able to make the paradigm shift necessary to survive. They have a wealth of knowledge on markets, risk management, innovation of products, and particularly regulatory oversight, among other things. That is why I would prefer to see them make the necessary paradigm shift and start to move more rapidly toward technological advances, including screen trading to replace the floors as we see them today.

I will come back to your thoughts on regulation later, but under your second scenario it sounded like you see a place for some type of floor?

Mollner: I believe that, given a good long-range plan, the exchanges have the ability to survive. As I stated, I also believe it would be best for the industry if they were the surviving entities.

Let me give you some of my thoughts on how this should be done. First, the exchanges and their membership have to realize that change is inevitable and to resist is to die. The membership must stop viewing technology as a threat and start to work with staff on how to improve the current method of handling orders. They must make dramatic strides toward cutting down on the processing of trades.

To me, this can be overly simplified by merely setting a goal to have the necessary information on an order entered only one time and that is by the first person who has it. Staff must step back and take a look at what they have and what is available in the market today. So much has changed that to "champion" a legacy system started 3, 5, or even 10 years ago is a terrible waste. A lot of what is available and being worked on should just be thrown out and started over. That requires tough decisions, but they must be made.

Although many believe the big liquid pits have a chance of surviving longer, it is evident that those are the ones that will come under attack first. They are also the markets where personal costs are so evident. You only have to look at the Eurodollar or T-bond pit to recognize that these markets are too people-intensive.

For years the futures commission merchants (FCMs) have asked that some of the new contracts that don't appear to have the immediate potential of being a large success be started on the exchange screens. I believe a transition of smaller markets to screens and floor traders moving into the bigger pits (even improving the liquidity) would have allowed everyone an opportunity to watch screen-based trading grow. It would also have been a good testing ground for the exchanges as they developed their system. The success of the E-Mini, which trades alongside the S&P 500 Index, makes one start to think about other such markets that provide local trading opportunities for the floor trader.

My thoughts are not always well-received, and I hear comments about some traders who don't believe they should have to change or give up their particular market, etc. It is that kind of thinking that puts the markets in jeopardy.

Given that you believe we will be screen trading in, say, 5 years, who will have the advantage, if any—the institutional trader or the speculator, be they large or small?

Mollner: Traders are traders. I have seen good and bad in both areas. It is generally believed, however, that the institutional trader has better information, which I do believe is true. They have access to more information and are in a better position to see order flow in the cash markets. But that is true today in our open-outcry markets.

Screen trading will take away some of the time advantage that is now available to the institutional trader, however. I would venture to say that most institutional traders have direct phone lines to the floor or to an upstairs broker who is in direct contact with the floor. That is not true with a retail order and even some large fund managers. Their orders are generally sent to the floor in a number of steps, which results in time delays. Those delays will be eliminated when everyone has access to screens. The delays will then be a result of systems and computer power and location, but the differences in access to the markets between retail and institutional orders will narrow considerably.

Okay, I'll buy that, but what happens to the order filler and the locals who are making their livings on the floor?

Mollner: Locals or independent traders are successful because they know how to trade and control their risk. The position traders will merely move upstairs; the scalpers and spreaders will have a more difficult time making the transition.

One of the largest traders on the Deutsche Terminbörse is in Chicago. Before trading from home on an exchange in Germany, he was a local in the T-bond pit. I have talked to some locals who now trade the E-mini and not only say they like it but almost immediately predicted screens will be coming faster than the floor population believes. Good traders are good traders, and they will adapt and move to screens.

As for the order filler, I believe most will become extinct. Some will become traders, but most will need to find new professions. Those on the floor who handle customer business will be affected by the changes.

So where do you see the industry going? Or, to be more precise, what will this business look like in, say, 5 to 10 years?

Mollner: Let me paint a picture 10 years out because I think the 5-year picture will still be in the making.

- First, the trading floors will be gone. They will have gone through some sort of metamorphosis during the period, but they won't be here 10 years from now.
- There will be one exchange in Chicago and one in New York. The entities will have merged to further reduce the

cost of trading, realizing that the large staffs necessary to support a large trading floor will no longer be needed.

- The only things remaining at the exchange, therefore, will be general administration, legal and compliance, new product development, and systems development.
- Clearing will be done by a separate clearing organization.
- On the client side there will be the institutional users, the individual retail speculator, and the large pool operators and commodity trading advisors. In addition, there will be a migration of the local trading community that will be trading from offices. All these participants will have basically the same computer access to the markets. The larger users will, of course, be networked into many markets as well as their separate analytical systems for risk control.
- A lot of the regulatory time that is now spent on trading floor issues will be shifted to client protection from trading oversight. With ease of access through the Internet, the small individual speculator will require that the regulatory body oversee futures issues such as sales practices and fraud.
- Speaking of regulators, 10 years from now we will have completely overhauled the financial services industries regulatory scheme. We currently have duplicative and, in some cases, multiple regulatory oversight in each market, with more than 10 federal and state agencies overseeing the various aspects of financial services. Just as we are seeing consolidation in the industry, I believe good business judgment will eventually overcome the political aspects of regulation, and we will see consolidation there also.

You mentioned a single clearinghouse. The exchanges in Chicago are talking about joining into a single clearing organization. Do you feel this is an important step?

Mollner: Although still in the formation stage, it is evident to all that there is a considerable savings to the industry. The total effect represents savings, but the displacements and political nature of the two Chicago exchanges make it a more difficult task than it need be.

Everyone now recognizes that the clearing process is a utility function and that the risk management aspects are for the protection of the clearing members and their customers. It is not necessary to have separate and competing organizations. In my years in the business, I rarely had a customer ask me about clearing. More important, no customer ever asked to trade on one exchange and clear at another. Clients either don't know or don't care; therefore, there is no benefit to either the exchange or the clearing members to pay for supporting duplicative organizations.

In addition to the obvious savings, there is what I refer to as the soft-dollar savings. For example, inside the large full-service firm, be it a securities firm or a bank, only so many resources in the technology department can be devoted to futures projects. If your head count is used for maintenance and new duplicative projects, your staff can't spend the time on new cost-saving and/or risk management systems. Senior management in all firms is cognizant of this problem.

The importance comes from the message that a movement toward common clearing will send to the major users and FCMs—that is, the exchanges recognize that the world is changing and they must reduce the costs of trading to remain competitive. To not do common clearing will send such a bad message that I believe it would not even be repairable. If it is not accomplished now, it won't be until after 2000, and by then those who make the decisions will be in the process of moving their business elsewhere.

EMERGING INTO THE FUTURE

James E. Oliff
Second Vice Chairman
Chicago Mercantile Exchange
Executive Director
International Futures & Options Associates

James E. Oliff, an attorney, has been involved in the futures industry for more than 30 years and is a second-generation member of the Chicago Mercantile Exchange (CME). He has experience in back office and floor operations and as an account executive in addition to serving a number of years on the CME board of directors.

He was elected second vice chairman of the CME in 1998 in the middle of his second consecutive term on the exchange board. He previously served on the board from 1985 to 1992 and was its second vice chairman from 1990 to 1992 and secretary in 1996.

Oliff has served in a number of roles at the exchange, including supervising the exchange's strategic planning efforts as chairman of the Strategic Planning Committee. He is also the chairman of the Regulatory Oversight, Business Conduct, Trading Floor Issues, Professional Responsibilities, and Gratuity Fund committees. He is cochairman of the Foreign Currency Committee and vice chairman of the Clearing House, Education, Financial Instrument Oversight, Emerging Market, and Member Services committees.

Oliff also is responsible for the development of the exchange's ethics program, the first such exchange program required of both members and employees in the futures industry. He has spoken on the subject of rule enforcement and professional responsibility in numerous forums and is a visiting lecturer in financial market ethics in the Graduate School of International Economics and Finance at Brandeis University in Waltham, Mass.

The executive director of International Futures and Options Associates, a broker association, Oliff also is the president of FILO Corporation.

Technology is probably the major issue that all sectors of the futures industry will have to deal with in the next few years. How do you think technology will affect exchanges, brokers, and traders in the future?

Oliff: The entire world is revolutionizing because of technology. Clearly, the futures industry is no different. That will take many forms. What is clear is that communications are possible in nanoseconds, and consequently, typical forms of brokerage activity are being drastically altered. Individuals are now capable of utilizing computers and communications networks to make their own trading decisions, and the trend for the future is for greater disintermediation. With online banking, the wide dissemination of products and services over the Internet, and the ease of establishing an electronic relationship, the traditional notions of customer loyalty have been changed forever. Typical brokerage firms that have relied on selling advice and having long-term, concrete relationships with customers will only be as good as their last recommendation and their last trade.

This clearly has a significant impact on futures exchanges and the entire futures brokerage business. Over the immediate term, more customers will be communicating directly with exchanges, either by telephone to the broker on the floor or by computer linkups provided by either the exchanges or brokerage firms or broker associations.

The only thing missing from the equation is whether the essential matching element will be computerized or whether that can still be done by human contact. With human interchange, you can direct the attention of the market participants to a particular area, see the panic in someone's eyes, and can hear and feel the excitement of the market. To me, that indicates that open outcry clearly produces the best form of price discovery and will survive longer than most people are currently assuming.

However, electronic trade does offer many advantages. It is cheaper, faster, less cumbersome, perceived to be more honest, and gives customers greater control over their trading activities. For many large benchmark products, such as the German bund and other interest rate products, customers will prefer the electronic option over open outcry. Likewise, for smaller products where there is little volume or volatility, simple laws of economics will dictate that the screen is preferred. For products where there is customer interest, significant volatility, and a reliance on the exchange of information, open outcry will survive much longer.

What is certain, however, is that the customer will drive the decision making, not the exchanges. Those exchanges that listen and respond to their customers and that can provide the platform and machinery first will be the exchanges that evolve into the twenty-first century most successfully.

How do you see the electronic process shaping up for order routing and handling?

Oliff: I see exchanges and order entry altering, depending on the type of investor. The small retail customer will be dealing directly via the Internet. Online trading not only for securities but also for futures will be the norm. Once the U.S. stock market stops going straight up and behaving like an odometer in a car— when stock returns are no longer superior and assured—much of that capital out there will look for other venues to reap a better return. Futures markets will become a logical alternative. The more product that can be tailored to appeal to that retail customer, the better positioned an exchange is and the better the exchange's chance for survival.

It would seem to me that the CME is properly positioned. We began positioning ourselves with the E-mini S&P contract, and I think you will see more "mini" contracts offered electronically. Such an approach accomplishes many things: It benefits the small, retail customer, it provides a vehicle for many market-makers to slowly make the transition to an electronic platform, and, by virtue of side-by-side trading with the larger market, it assists the larger market in disseminating its bids, offers, and indications of market depth.

As for the larger institutional customers, I think you will see order-entry systems directly in the hands of the ultimate customer. They will be able to view a market and input an order directly into a trading system that will probably be routed intermediately through a clearing member for credit-checking purposes. All that will happen in a nanosecond. Once the trade is made and matched, not only will it have been delivered electronically, but it will be reported electronically at the same time to the exchange, the clearing member, and the customer.

How is Globex$_2$ fitting into the process to facilitate trading?

Oliff: Globex$_2$ is properly structured to provide the order-entry and order-routing functions directly into a broker's terminal so trades can be made electronically. Globex$_2$ is an essential part of a trading network and can also provide the back-end matching engine. It differs from the first-generation Globex by accommodating specific types of orders, and its platform is expansive and ultimately will be able to be utilized on any PC. So the distribution of Globex$_2$ will be much greater, and its trading techniques and engine will be much more readily adaptable. Of course, it will have to crawl before it can walk, and it will have to walk before it can run, but it gives us the platform and the adaptability to handle trading in the future

The key for the future, I think, is the ability to handle many things on one platform. Nobody wants to have six or seven different trading systems on their desk. They want just one system where they can not only do their personal bookkeeping or access the Internet but also deal with their trading. An adaptable system is the best. The question is who is going to control that software and who is going to control access to the network. But, in any case, it has to be readily available and easy to use.

How will the transition to more automated trading affect the brokerage business? How will the broker's role change?

Oliff: In the securities industry you have already seen a change. So many online brokerage services are appearing on almost a daily basis that you would be foolish not to assume that would extend into the futures industry as well. At the same time that is occurring, your regular full-service brokerage firms still provide a useful function. There will always be those who are willing to pay for particular advice or sophisticated trading strategies, and that will be balanced against those who want to make their own trading decisions.

As for the brokerage business in general, brokerage firms will continue to play an essential role, and exchanges will continue to rely on them not only for distribution but also to provide the necessary credit function.

What will happen to the floor trader?

Oliff: Floor traders are a remarkable breed. They have the uncanny ability to adapt to changing trading situations and find a way to make a good living. The change in trading platform is just that—a situation change to which the trader can adapt. That is not to suggest that it will be an easy decision or transition, but it can be done. Whether it is open outcry or electronic, the floor trader will continue to function as a market-maker and an essential liquidity provider. What floor traders give up in terms of proximity to order flow can be replaced by the advantage of having many markets and sources of information at their immediate disposal.

Floor brokers will also continue to have a function in the electronic age. Many investors don't want to be tied down to a screen all day; others will continue to have complicated trading strategies and find worthwhile the benefits of discretion and professionalism that floor brokers provide. Likewise, many institutions will not want their traders to assume the execution risk and will continue to pay for such services.

As I look at my children, it is clear the computer is their best friend. I joke with my wife that the only way I can talk to my teenager these days is through e-mail. They have complete faith and trust in using the computer. So what we are looking at is a generational issue and transition. We are one generation away from having computer-literate people controlling the trading platforms and feeling comfortable trading on them. What is essential for the short term is finding a way to manage that transition successfully. As many traders migrate gradually to the computer and as the trade becomes ready for the next generation, those traders will need to be equipped and made to feel comfortable with the computer as a trading vehicle.

One of the features that is coming out of this transition in trading is the matter of exchange ownership that has been raised at the CME, the London International Financial Futures Exchange, and elsewhere. What is your view on the future of exchanges and how they will develop in light of the sensitive political realities that need to be addressed?

Oliff: I think exchanges will be increasingly pressured to provide not only markets but also revenue sources for their membership. What is often ignored is that seat prices should reflect member opportunity. To the extent that electronic trading systems pose a challenge to traditional exchanges and the traditional roles that members of exchanges use to realize income, there is obviously a pressure on membership prices. Exchanges will need to find new revenue-generating opportunities in any new electronic business system in order to enhance member opportunity.

Likewise, some exchanges will seek to restructure from a membership organization to a for-profit entity. Members will be able to capture revenue from these new opportunities and will continue to receive benefits in the form of reduced transaction and access costs that justify today's membership prices; additional benefits such as access to the book or other preferences will also enhance membership value.

What additional services will exchanges be able to provide to attract even more business?

Oliff: Exchanges offer transparency, liquidity, creditworthiness, and anonymity. Those things fall in and out of favor. To the extent that the derivatives market becomes more and more plain vanilla, it would seem to me that exchanges will provide a necessary function.

First, exchange prices are transparent. I would think that exchange prices could be utilized in a much more effective way as a reference price for many of the tailored derivative transactions that occur. For example, it has become increasingly common in the currency market to have "knockout" currency derivatives, caps, and collars where it is absolutely essential that there be a viable reference price. It would seem that futures prices could perform that function for many of these tailored derivatives products.

The Russian ruble is a case in point. The CME is now publishing the CME/EMTA Russian Ruble Reference price that is being used by the derivatives community as the standard to which most ruble derivatives contracts settle. Other opportunities will certainly present themselves.

Second, exchanges offer a pool of liquidity providers, and it is a lot easier for an individual to find multiple counterparties on one specific trading platform.

Finally, to the extent that exchanges help to eliminate counterparty risk, I think you will see many exchanges start to offer products where counterparty risk clearly needs to be mitigated. This is envisioned by the Merc's movement into the emerging markets. Having a stable and reliable counterparty to each transaction is clearly desired by the derivatives community.

I would say that exchanges can continue to survive and function very well simply by providing those tools that they presently utilize but finding a way to capitalize on what their definite strengths are to the interbank market.

At the present time with all the megamergers taking place, nobody seems to be really concerned about credit-worthiness. But everything has its cycles, and I think there will come a time in the not-too-distant future when credit-worthiness will once again become a major issue. It's not an immediate issue, but at any time its importance can become major. The question is whether or not you can survive during that period of time when nobody thinks you're relevant.

Other services such as cross-margining, clearing, common banking, information, and customizing all of that to particular users offer attractive possibilities. Finally, the exchange as the owner of the trading platform and network need no longer be simply a futures exchange. It can offer cash products, securities, financing, and other services on its platform that add value.

How do you think the introduction of the Euro will affect currency trading at the CME over the longer term?

Oliff: The CME obviously is well-positioned in its currency complex. Most of the currencies we offer are not affected by any European Union. Gradually, what you will see is the D-mark pit being swallowed up by the Euro. So, to that extent, the exchange is probably not materially affected.

To the extent that we may end up having two major reserve international currencies and that many commodities—gold, oil, etc.—typically quoted in dollars are quoted in other terms, I think that successful European unity promises more opportunity than threat to many exchanges.

One of the areas of the world with which you are quite familiar is Latin America. What impact will Latin America have on futures trading?

Oliff: I am a firm believer that one of the major niches that the CME should be pursuing is emerging markets. I currently trade, as well as broker, all of the emerging market products. I see all of the advantages of futures exchanges coming to play in the emerging markets. To the extent that we can increase price transparency and, by doing that, possibly prevent panic and chaos, I think the future of exchanges is very bright if they continue to increase emerging market business, and I think the value of their contribution is readily apparent.

The situation of the Russian ruble is a case in point. Whatever argument you can make for that market can be applied to almost any emerging market. Obviously, for us in Chicago the Latin American economies made a great deal of sense because we were not dealing with serious time lags, and open outcry was a nice fit. As the platform becomes electronic, more of the world opens. We can focus on worldwide relationships and the role of the emerging markets within them.

Many fine futures exchanges already exist in Latin America. The BM&F (Bolsa de Mercadorias & Futures) in Sao Paulo is extremely advanced technologically and is a very sophisticated exchange. I think it is essential for the Merc and major U.S. exchanges to make overtures there and figure out ways to strategically align and share common trading platforms and not be seen as attempting to take away national forms of risk management. It is essential we find ways to cooperate and work together.

What are other emerging market areas that might at-tract the attention of currency and stock index traders in the future?

Oliff: Oh, my, I don't even know where to begin. Poland, Tur-key, Israel, India, Korea, Argentina, Greece . . . those are some countries where there clearly is international investment inter-est, and finding some common risk management platform would be extremely valuable.

What current market areas are most vulnerable to change in the next 5 to 10 years—areas that will grow or areas that might disappear?

Oliff: I think credit derivatives and finding ways to standardize credit exposure are going to be a major challenge. CO_2 emission permits and other forms of pollution control devices are going to become very important as we move into the twenty-first century. What will ultimately happen as the world relies more on com-munication and the Internet to transact business is that people will move to where the quality of life is the best. As qual-ity-of-life issues take on increasing importance, I would think pollution and control of pollution will become especially impor-tant. Likewise, catastrophe and weather futures will come to play an increasingly important role, both in the area of risk man-agement and in enhancing diversification and returns in portfo-lio management.

In terms of computerization changing how we trade now, in-terest rate contracts are probably a lot more vulnerable than the currencies. I think you will see them migrating to an electronic platform faster than other things. Open outcry will continue to function in traditional commodity markets—grains, livestock, metals, etc.

One proposal related to that issue is that the two Chi-cago exchanges merge, one trading agricultural prod-

ucts and the other financial products. How do you react to that idea?

Oliff: Clearly, an attractive case can be made. To the extent that open outcry remains vibrant, combining exchanges produces trading synergies and economies of scale that cannot be ignored. On an electronic platform, everybody wants to provide enough product that it can enhance the platform's distribution. In the financial arena, combining both the short and long end of the curve makes the Board of Trade a logical partner for the CME as well. Finally, the significance of both exchanges to our common members and the economic community of Chicago cannot be ignored.

The exchanges must consider combining, but that requires that they also share a common vision for the future to make that happen. At the same time, each exchange will be pursuing other partners and alliances to ensure that any electronic platform has the necessary product, technology, and distribution to provide its membership with ample opportunity to trade and prosper. In the end, it may be those additional partnerships and alliances that help combine the two entities.

To summarize, what is the one issue or development that you see as the most significant for the futures industry and traders in the next 5 to 10 years?

Oliff: For the futures industry as a whole, finding a regulatory platform that is truly international will be the biggest issue to face. As you adapt to electronic and Internet trade, the need for international standards will become increasingly apparent.

For the individual investor, the ability to adapt to technological change and its speed and to get those delivery tools readily available will be the biggest opportunity—and the biggest challenge.

THE FRENCH EXPERIENCE

Gérard Pfauwadel
Former Chairman and Chief Executive Officer
Marché a Terme International de France

Gérard Pfauwadel was named chairman and chief executive officer of Matif S.A. on June 14, 1988, and chairman of the Banque Centrale de Compensation, B.C.C. (Commodities Futures Clearing House) on January 4, 1990. He guided Matif's development into one of the world's major futures exchanges for 10 years before resigning in April 1998.

Prior to leading the Matif, Pfauwadel's career in the French Treasury from 1976 to 1988 included positions as secretary of the Paris Club from 1976 to 1980; project manager at Union d'Etudes et d'Investissement (Crédit Agricole), 1981 to 1982; chief of the cabinet of permanent Under-Secretary of the Treasury Michel Camdessus, 1982 to 1983; general secretary of the C.I.R.L. (industrial restructuring), 1984 to 1985; and Deputy Under-Secretary of the French Treasury in charge of financial markets, 1986 to 1988.

He has also served on a number of committees related to business, futures/options industry, and exchange matters.

Matif made one of the most dramatic transitions in futures trading ever seen in the spring of 1998, moving

from floor trading to electronic trading completely within just a couple of months. How did this happen so quickly, and what does it suggest for other exchanges?

Pfauwadel: Global business, fierce competition, and demand for an easy, secure, flexible, and cost-effective way of trading led naturally to electronic trading. Matif clearly was ready for such a mutation.

All the markets created in the late 1980s were electronic markets. Right now, it terms of numbers of derivatives exchanges, the electronic ones are in the majority; in five years time they will represent the majority in volume as well.

What will these developments mean for the brokerage business in Europe?

Pfauwadel: The first key element that will affect everything in Europe, of course, is the advent of the Euro. Linked with the takeoff of electronic trading, there will be fewer instruments (due to the disappearance of the domestic currencies) but also a more intensive use of Euro-denominated derivatives products. The Euro yield curve and stock index products will be very much in demand, and the size of their markets will rival the corresponding U.S. dollar-denominated markets.

So we will certainly see a concentration effort in the brokerage business to benefit from economy of scales from firms that will be able to offer customers the whole range of products of Euroland.

How will these developments affect your institutional and retail traders?

Pfauwadel: They should affect institutional or retail traders in the same manner by reducing their costs to have access to markets and by offering a more secure track record of their orders and executions.

What new product or service innovations will exchanges offer traders in the next 5 to 10 years?

Pfauwadel: The field for offering futures is very broad. Everywhere there is risk. Some people are against it, and others are ready to bear it. It would be too ambitious an undertaking to describe all the possible underlying innovative products, but observe the Chicago Board of Trade's attempts with insurance, pollution allowance, etc.

In addition to the very innovative products that might be developed, one thing it is possible for exchanges to do more readily is to improve service offered on the plain-vanilla products—links with over-the-counter markets, cash markets, clearing services. . . .

In this picture what is the outlook for international exchange linkages?

Pfauwadel: Technology improvements mean large investments for the exchanges. It seems that in the future we will see more and more linkages based on technology agreements to share in those large investments. The FCMs (futures commission merchants) will encourage exchanges to do so because they know that at the end of the day they pay for these investments with their fees.

A few standards will emerge in terms of trading and clearing engines. NSC/Clearing 21® is well-positioned to become one of those standards. For the front end, it is possible that the move to standardization will be even more integrative and that, finally, one or two main standards could be the universal way to have access to all the main derivatives markets in the world.

Regarding networks, it seems that situation is even more open, with potential exchange networks, FCM networks, the Internet, and other possibilities.

Matif is already involved in a number of alliances and groups. How do you see the exchange fitting into Europe's and the world's financial marketplace?

Pfauwadel: Matif inside the European Economic and Monetary Union (EMU) will play on the Euro yield curve. In the fixed-income business, Matif will offer a complete service for trading and clearing in the cash, repo, and derivatives markets.

Inside the SBF Group, Matif will use and promote the NSC/GL/Clearing 21® standard. Matif, within its alliance network (Eurex, South Europe exchanges, Chicago Mercantile Exchange, etc.), will broaden the membership having access to its products.

As a commodity exchange, Matif will pursue its diversification with notable agricultural products, which should really take off with the reduction of the Common Agricultural Policy.

Moving away from electronic trading and exchange issues for the moment to the trading world in general, how do you see technology shaping the futures and options industry and the way people trade in the next few years?

Pfauwadel: Order routing, order entry, technical relationships with customers, better control of risk with a priori credit control devices . . . , there are many ways technology will influence trading. The most important is certainly the fact that this technology progress in trading, as in other human activity, will permit industry participants to do their business more easily and in a more cost-effective manner. This reduces the cost to enter into the market and increases competition, which normally should benefit customers.

What markets are most vulnerable to change in this environment?

Pfauwadel: Again, due to technology progress, globalization, and competition, all the markets that are not really disintermediated. The equity markets will change a lot in the years to come. A global economy calls for global investments and global investors. There will be many changes in terms of competitive listings, access, and services.

Is there one issue that stands out as a challenge to exchanges?

Pfauwadel: For regulated markets such as Matif, it is the competition with OTC business.

POSITIONING IN NEW YORK

Daniel Rappaport
Chairman and Chief Executive Officer
New York Mercantile Exchange

D aniel Rappaport, chairman of the board and chief executive officer of the New York Mercantile Exchange (NYMEX), has been chairman of the exchange since 1993 and a member of the board of directors since 1986.

During his tenure as chairman, Rappaport has successfully orchestrated a $71 million merger deal with Commodity Exchange Inc. (Comex), the world's largest precious metals exchange, and a relocation of NYMEX to new facilities. He planned, negotiated, and supervised the development and construction of the exchange's new 500,000 square foot corporate headquarters in lower Manhattan, completing the project on time and under budget at a cost of $215 million.

Prior to joining NYMEX, Rappaport worked for a law firm engaged in the practice of general corporate law.

He serves as a member of the National Petroleum Council and is also on the board of trustees of New York Law School. Rappaport received two special service awards in 1997—the Ellis Island Medal of Honor for his service to the community and the Distinguished Service Award from the 100 Year Association of New York for his service to the financial community.

The New York Mercantile Exchange has been a center of attention in the futures industry with mergers, new floor facilities, electronic trading with ACCESS, exchange linkages, volatile markets. . . . From your perspective, what are the major challenges NYMEX will face in the next 5 to 10 years?

Rappaport: Our merger with Comex, the use of electronic trading, and linkage partners in the Far East have been key to the continued growth and internationalization of NYMEX. Additionally, since we moved to our state-of-the-art trading facility in the summer of 1997, we have seen a tremendous increase in our trading volumes and, at the same time, a dramatic drop in our error rates. All of these accomplishments have laid the foundation for our continued growth into the future. However, major challenges do lie ahead for all exchanges, and we recognize that we constantly need to look at our business and the business of our customers and be able to adapt to changes in the marketplace.

The continued evolution of technology, particularly its application on the trading floor, the evolution of electronic trading, and our relationship with over-the-counter (OTC) derivative dealers will continue to drive changes in our business. We will look at the opportunity to utilize technology and electronic trading on our trading floor to reduce costs to our members and their customers while simultaneously increasing the liquidity in our existing products and the availability of new products and services.

What is NYMEX doing to develop electronic trading?

Rappaport: We are currently cooperating with the International Petroleum Exchange (IPE) in the development of our next-generation electronic trading system, NYMEX ACCESS 2000. This system will give NYMEX the premier electronic trading system for our energy and metals products. This system, coupled with our relationship with the IPE, our linkage partners in the Far East, and the development of a Far East crude oil contract, should enable us to better serve our members, customers, and OTC dealers.

Of those items you mentioned, which do you see as the single most important issue or development that will affect individual traders in the next five years?

Rappaport: As can be seen from the recent announcements by LIFFE (London International Financial Futures and Options Exchange), SFE (Sydney Futures Exchange), HKFE (Hong Kong Futures Exchange), and alliances such as Eurex—the electronic alliance between the DTB (Deutsche Terminbörse) and Swiss Options and Financial Futures Exchange—the single most important issue that will affect individual traders in the next five years clearly is technology and advances in electronic trading. As an exchange, we will continue to look at the automation of processes using systems such as electronic trading, order routing, and small-order execution, with open standards, to enhance and augment the efficiency of our open-outcry markets.

How do you think order routing and trade execution will change, if at all, as we move into the next century?

Rappaport: I think you will see more automated handling of small orders—one and two lots—to reduce handling costs. Links between routing systems and other electronic trading networks will be programmed to allow a single point of entry into a ubiquitous, transparent system for traders anywhere on the planet. New technologies that bring remote traders closer to the pits, such as virtual reality or other broadband communications, will be adopted. Execution of the electronic orders will require development of automated forms of liquidity support.

How will this affect the retail trader, brokers, floor traders?

Rappaport: Retail traders will find it difficult to transact business outside the technological systems. The cost of handling their business manually is too high. It is incumbent on exchanges to create—conceptually and physically—a technological infrastructure that will keep the open-outcry system of trading economically and functionally competitive with the evolving electronic trading environment. The ultimate objective should be to have a floor staff that is exclusively composed of floor brokers who electronically communicate (written and oral) with their back office.

In this changing environment, what contracts or markets are the most vulnerable to change in the next 5 to 10 years?

Rappaport: Today it appears the financial instrument-based markets are more at risk than physical commodity markets because the participants in the debt, equity, interest rate, and currency markets use screens to facilitate their transactions as a normal course of business. Moreover, the larger the universe of market participants, the more susceptible the market is to the risks of becoming completely dominated by electronic trading.

The converse is also true: The smaller the universe of market participants, the more the market is compelled to rely upon the floor community of market-makers to provide depth of market liquidity.

Look at the CME's trading of the S&P 500 Index E-mini contract or Cantor Fitzgerald's electronic Cantor Exchange to trade cash bonds and futures on the underlying instruments. This trend toward electronic trading is underscored by the recently announced plans by the SFE and HKFE, which trade primarily financial products, to close their floors within the next 12 to 18 months. Also, DTB, an electronic exchange, successfully captured market share in the bund contract from LIFFE by providing lower-cost automated execution of the contract.

In the longer term, all markets are vulnerable to change, and I believe we are well-positioned with our NYMEX ACCESS

2000 system to deliver our products in any mode or format demanded by our members and their customers.

How will the new New York Board of Trade and its relationship with Cantor Fitzgerald affect NYMEX traders?

Rappaport: The announcement by Cantor to begin trading a Treasury bond contract in direct competition with the Chicago Board of Trade raised our awareness that electronics and technology could make it easier than ever for a competitor to attempt to take away our market share. As a result, we have been working diligently to bring new technologies, such as wireless technology and hand-held terminals, to the floor to improve the efficiency of our open-outcry execution system.

We also are in the process of developing our next-generation electronic trading system, NYMEX ACCESS 2000, which will have 24-hour trading capabilities and will provide us with the flexibility to list more of our products on the screen during the day or those of other exchanges should our customers want it.

In addition, we will continue to work with our customers to provide the products and execution services they demand in a cost-efficient environment so that, in the event a competitor does emerge, our customers will choose to remain loyal to NYMEX because of the cost-effective, flexible environment we offer to facilitate their trading and risk management needs.

How do recent exchange mergers, such as Nasdaq and the American Stock Exchange (AMEX), affect your exchange?

Rappaport: The Nasdaq-AMEX merger is another in a series of consolidations and alliances sweeping the industry—a trend that began with our merger with the Comex back in 1994. I believe this trend will continue, as is evident by the Eurex alliance.

At NYMEX we have several linkage arrangements in place, including our linkages with the Hong Kong Futures Exchange and the Sydney Futures Exchange, to diversify our customer base and build trading opportunities for our members and their customers. In addition, as I mentioned earlier, we have been co-operating with the IPE in building our ACCESS 2000 system, and we are working on a strategic alliance that will offer a diverse set of energy trading and risk management opportunities to our respective members and customers through our global distribution network.

What changes do you see, if any, in the way New York exchanges disseminate price quotes and data to retail traders?

Rappaport: Retail traders can get our real-time or delayed quotes through a market data vendor or via the Internet today. This provides flexibility to the marketplace to meet the traders' needs. It is my belief that we will see continued movement to open standard interfaces and an increased reliance on the Internet for dissemination of our market data. These advances should be a win-win situation for exchanges and traders who rely on the data. Although this will reduce the actual cost of the data to the trader, the fact that the data itself will become more of a commodity will be of huge benefit to the exchange.

How will New York's role as a major center for pricing and trading energy, metals, and softs change in the next 5 to 10 years?

Rappaport: NYMEX will continue to provide the most liquid markets for risk management and transparent price discovery for energy and metals. Our role as a global leader for energy and metals trading will continue with the rollout of new and innovative products such as aluminum, coal, electricity, and a Far East crude oil contract. In addition, with the creation of NYMEX ACCESS 2000 and the expanded capacity of our new state-of-the-art trading facility, we have the flexibility to trade our products 24 hours a day in the most liquid forum, as demanded by our members and customers.

How would common clearing benefit the futures industry, brokerage firms, and traders?

Rappaport: The direct benefit is cost reduction. First, for our futures commission merchants and proprietary clearing members, it will provide a single interface and operating procedure that is less expensive to manage. Second, for traders, common clearing leads to reduced margin requirements and costs of doing business.

Exchanges based in London have enjoyed a significant competitive advantage over their global competitors due to their participation in the London Clearing House (LCH). The LCH has made a major contribution to the reduced cost of doing business in London.

In the long term I would like to see a common U.S.-based clearinghouse that would link up through a common banking agreement with European- and Asian-based common clearing entities to provide a global network of common clearing.

With our rollout of Clearing 21 this year, a clearing system that we jointly developed with the Chicago Mercantile Exchange, we will have a state-of-the-art clearing system that we expect could become the global industry standard.

What about international exchange linkages beyond common clearing?

Rappaport: The trend, as I see it, will continue toward exchange linkages and mergers. As technology continues to evolve, the cost of constructing these linkages will be reduced. Our linkages have been cost-effective vehicles to expand our products and services into new markets and time zones. In addition, these linkages will enable our members to access new and diverse products through cross-border trading arrangements.

The direct benefit to our members will be an increase in their trading opportunities. Traders will, therefore, have better opportunities to find market niches based on unique linkage-based strategies.

One final question that seems to be on everyone's minds: How will the Year 2000 (Y2K) computer issue affect your exchange, the futures industry, and traders?

Rappaport: Y2K is a huge issue for all industries. For NYMEX, Y2K computer maintenance drains exchange resources that could be applied to other projects. NYMEX has been an active participant with industry groups, such as the Futures Industry Association and the Securities Industry Association, in ensuring that the exchange and its members are Y2K compliant. Although the ramifications of this problem could be huge, the industry, the exchanges, and its members have taken steps to manage the risk properly.

THE COOPERATIVE WAY

Leslie Rosenthal
Managing Partner
Rosenthal Collins Group

Leslie Rosenthal, managing partner of Rosenthal Collins Group, a Chicago-based commodities firm, has been involved in exchange government since his election to the Chicago Board of Trade (CBOT) Board of Directors in 1974. He has served the CBOT in numerous capacities including consecutive one-year terms as exchange chairman in 1981 and 1982 after having been vice chairman of the exchange in 1979 and chairman of the Board of Trade Clearing Corporation in 1980.

In 1975 he was instrumental in pioneering the start of trading in interest rate futures at the CBOT. Over the years he has chaired many CBOT committees, including Financial Instruments, New Products, Commodity Options, and Finance, and has been a member of the exchange's Executive, Member Services, Public Relations, Floor Practices, Membership, and Margin committees. He has also served on the governing boards of the Chicago Mercantile Exchange (CME), the International Monetary Market (IMM) at the CME, and the MidAmerica Commodity Exchange.

Rosenthal became a CBOT member in 1958 after working on the exchange floor for seven years. For the next five years, he worked as a floor manager, market analyst, and in other capacities for two commodity firms, Lamson Brothers and Harris Upham &

Co. From 1963 to 1970 he was an independent trader, handling wheat orders for large Chicago brokerage houses.

You have been known for speaking your mind on exchange and futures industry issues. Considering mainly the interests of the trader, what decisions—by the exchanges, brokerage firms, government—have been most beneficial in the last 20 years?

Rosenthal: The policy of the futures industry over the years has been dictated by the major exchanges. The futures commission merchants and the U.S. government have only reacted to the decisions of the exchanges. The most beneficial decisions were the steps taken to expand the product base of the Chicago Mercantile Exchange and the Chicago Board of Trade in the late 1970s and early 1980s. Without the bond market at the CBOT and the IMM at the CME, we would not be at the forefront of an international marketplace.

On the other side of the coin, what are the biggest mistakes that have been made?

Rosenthal: The biggest mistakes have been in building fixed overhead and not expending enough capital for new products to take the place of our maturing financial contracts.

Regarding fixed overhead, does this relate to physical facilities such as the new trading floors at various exchanges or does it refer to the slowness in adapting to electronic trading or to the consolidation of exchange functions such as clearing?

Rosenthal: The new financial trading floor at the CBOT is a very significant piece of my criticism of fixed overhead, not because we spent $182 million to build a single-purpose building but because the financing at this stage in our life basically has managed to squeeze out anything we would have in the way of cash or assets to throw at new products coming along or even adapting to electronic trading. So I think it's a fair assessment that, if we hadn't spent that much money on the building, we would be able to allocate our resources to some of these other threats of competition that are coming our way.

A number of exchange mergers and alliances have already been announced in 1998—New York Board of Trade, Eurex, Chicago Board Options Exchange-Pacific Stock Exchange, Nasdaq-American Stock Exchange-Philadelphia Stock Exchange, to name a few. Now the signs seem to be increasing that maybe even the CBOT and the CME could merge. What are your views on this possibility, and what does it portend for traders?

Rosenthal: It's a natural consideration for the Chicago exchanges to be arm in arm on some type of a common electronic platform in alliance with a strong European partner. But there is a hurdle we have to get over. The CBOT is involved in an agreement with the DTB/Eurex, and the CME is already committed to an electronic platform that was developed in conjunction with a French partner. At this date neither side wants to abandon their initiatives. So it looks like the merger, although everybody agrees it would be a good thing and it probably has legs because of the competitive threat that we have now that we didn't have in the past, seems to be dead on arrival because the two exchanges can't agree on what electronic system they should adopt.

Is that a resolvable issue or is it likely to remain a roadblock for some time?

Rosenthal: Well, somebody's got to give up, and in our industry it's very difficult to get one side or the other to say, "Okay, I'll adopt your approach." We are all very competitive animals.

Regarding new products, the exchanges have introduced contracts on various stock indexes—specifically, the Dow Jones contracts at the CBOT—insurance, electricity, and other "commodities." What is your view of these new products? In what new products should the exchanges be investing money instead of putting it into fixed overhead?

Rosenthal: I think the problem we have is that the Chicago exchanges are looking for a home-run like the CBOT had in the bond contract or the CME had in the Eurodollars. I don't think there is such a thing on the horizon.

What we really should be looking for is a group of new products that might be considered a lesser success than those two big winners—anything that would add to our volume and give us some income is something we should consider. You have to throw a whole bunch of things against the wall and see what sticks. That includes the new electricity contracts, continuing to develop insurance, seeing if there is something we could do in the way of risk management, maybe developing something with a real estate index attached to it . . . all of these things.

Now, looking ahead, what do you see as the single most important futures industry issue or development for traders in the next 5 to 10 years?

Rosenthal: The most important issue will be the relationship between open outcry and screen trading. Does it develop on a competitive or cooperative level?

What does the rapid growth of screen trading internationally, especially in Europe, suggest for how we will trade futures in the future, considering the quick transition to screens at the Marché a Terme International de France, the bund shift from the London Inter-

national Financial Futures Exchange (LIFFE) to the Deutsche Terminbörse, LIFFE's automation plans, and other examples?

Rosenthal: The European exchanges' response to competition between open outcry and screen trading gets a little more complicated in Chicago. In Chicago we have a larger number of pit traders, a long-standing tradition, and exchange support for open outcry, and the ownership and makeup of the exchanges are different than they are in Europe.

One of the things everybody points to in Europe is the fact that the DTB, an electronic exchange, beat LIFFE, an open-outcry exchange, and won the German bund contract. People forget there was almost a nationalistic effort on the part of the German banks to win back the bund contract because the natural place for it to be trading is in Frankfurt rather than in London. That effort had a lot to do with the success of the electronic trading medium.

It's going to be a more bitter, longer fight in Chicago. To me it is unclear whether electronic trading will take over from open outcry or whether they will exist hand in hand. There is no doubt that electronic trading will take a measure of the volume, but I don't know if it is going to be a death blow.

What do you see as the ideal grand plan for developing open outcry and screen trading on a cooperative basis in the United States? How should this plan unfold, step by step?

Rosenthal: There ought to be some type of pilot or trial program for a side-by-side period—let's say for the next year or so. We have to be prepared at the Chicago exchanges to do something in the way of offering a screen-based trading alternative to the people who want to use it and then seeing what's happening a year from now. It's a moving target, as far as I'm concerned, and there is no finality as to which one is going to win out.

How else will the rapid expansion in technology affect brokerage firms and exchanges in the next 5 to 10 years?

Rosenthal: The advance of technology will push the brokerage firms to call for more consolidation of exchanges and clearing functions, and resistance will only hasten development of competitive screen-based trading systems.

How will order routing and trade execution take place as we move into the next century?

Rosenthal: Order routing and trade execution are becoming more automated each and every day. It is in this arena that the exchanges are doing their best job.

How do you see Project A developing?

Rosenthal: Project A at the CBOT is more accepted by floor traders than other trade-matching systems because it more closely resembles open outcry.

Do you think the liquidity in Project A or other screen trading will be sufficient to shift financial futures and options away from open-outcry trading in the next few years?

Rosenthal: Screen trading will shift some of the financial futures, but it is still not clear whether it will shift a significant enough amount to have it all move to screen trading. Project A is just another screen-trading mechanism. I think the jury is still out, at least in Chicago, on whether or not screen trading is a better way to go than open outcry.

How will the Cantor Fitzgerald proposal or other potential over-the-country "exchange" operations affect this situation?

Rosenthal: If I had to pick a serious competitor immediately for the CBOT, it would have been Cantor Fitzgerald because it has a valued and extensive customer base. So you couldn't have picked a bigger or better competitor. But, having said that, if you are successful in beating the biggest threat you have ever had, the story is over. If Cantor Fitzgerald can't take a significant volume from open outcry, nobody will succeed in taking a significant market share.

With all the changes taking place, what will be the role of the "traditional" broker and floor trader in the years ahead?

Rosenthal: The role of the traditional broker and floor trader will be dictated by the liquidity of the screen-trading systems. There are those who argue that open outcry will never die because the screens will be unable to duplicate the gathering of many individual traders into one central location to produce liquidity. I think this argument works better for traditional markets like grains and meats but not as well for financials.

How will the Internet affect how your customers get market information, data, etc.?

Rosenthal: The Internet obviously has cut back any information advantage "professional" traders had in the past, and now retail customers are close to an equal footing on breaking news items.

With screen trading, the Internet, etc., producing a more level information field, where will traders get their "edge" in the future?

Rosenthal: Traders will have to develop some type of proprietary software systems that allow them to execute multiple transactions at the same time. That is where they will get their edge. Instead of people poking at a screen, they will have to have some type of software that automates the transaction based on parameters they are able to feed into a computer that will execute the transactions together rather than execute the transactions one by one. It takes miniseconds to hit a key, but those miniseconds can make the difference in whether or not you get the trade executed.

The question will be what parameters you put into the computer, and everybody will have a different theory. That, therefore, will keep up the I-think-I-ought-to-buy/the-other-guy-thinks-he-ought-to-sell type of situations that characterize the markets. So it makes for divergent opinions although it might make for divergent opinions only on what the parameters should be.

Will firms such as yours be able to help traders in this regard?

Rosenthal: Yes, we are in the process of developing a system that allows traders to come off the floor into an office and have automated order entry and, we hope, some type of automated trading system where they can set the parameters and let the computer execute the trade for them. We are already starting to do this.

How will traders and brokerage firms deal with the trend toward global, round-the-clock trading?

Rosenthal: Only a relatively few retail customers trade around the clock, and only trading advisors seem to need these expanded trading outlets.

How can traders cope with the clout of the funds, which are often cited in the press as the factor behind price movements?

Rosenthal: The trading of futures funds will not have any permanent impact on the retail trader although the funds have some momentary price effect.

Would a two-tier market, with a different set of regulations for retail traders and institutional traders such as the funds, benefit retail traders?

Rosenthal: The exchanges seem to favor two-tier markets on a regulatory basis, but my belief is that it might damage the marketplace. You already have the criticism that our marketplace favors large traders with large ticket size at the expense of the small retail trader. Anything that you have that furthers that kind of contention hurts the marketplace because we rely on the small traders to keep our markets moving. Anything that puts them at a disadvantage obviously is not something I would favor. Everyone should be in one marketplace, as they have been.

What market areas are most vulnerable to change in the next 5 to 10 years?

Rosenthal: The success of the U.S. government in balancing the budget and paying down the debt would make the CBOT financial complex the most vulnerable to change.

I realize you can only guess like everyone else, but in your opinion, how realistic is it that the United States will balance the budget and pay down debt for any extended period?

Rosenthal: Part of the problem we are having in trading is that there isn't much volatility in the marketplace. Our traders need volatility. There isn't any "story" you can give to the trading public when interest rates are pretty static; there is no reason to even switch around between different maturities. On the one hand, the U.S. government has done a very good job over the last few years, but, on the other hand, it has certainly gone a long way toward hurting our markets. A blip in inflation would change it, but I'm not sure about getting it.

What would you say in a "pep talk" to encourage futures industry leaders as they look ahead? What would you warn them about?

Rosenthal: The futures industry is becoming a more acceptable asset class, and our markets have a larger customer base than ever before. Our markets are not "going away." It will be necessary, however, to have a more unified approach on the part of U.S. exchanges to meet the challenges of cost and foreign competition.

What factors are essential for this "unified approach"?

Rosenthal: A more unified approach is what circumstances are driving us toward already—that is, the Chicago exchanges together with some type of credible partner, whether it's European or Pacific Rim. The problem we now have is that everyone is looking at the Pacific Rim as a disaster area and, therefore, not looking to court any partners there. But putting together the European leg will automatically bring about a Pacific Rim partner as well somewhere else along the line in the next couple of years.

Anything else you would add to your "Here is what we need to do" message?

Rosenthal: The only other thing I can think of is that I belong in Scottsdale, Arizona, or retired drinking beer on a lake somewhere.

You probably are one of those people who will never "retire."

Rosenthal: Yeah, I suppose that's probably right. But, you know, I think it's remarkable that people are so depressed about our industry. Everybody feels threatened, so everybody is pretty far down in the mouth.

The thing you have to do is to encourage the people who are staring at what they see as a cannon in the face of open outcry. It's almost like getting the news about cancer. Somebody says you have been diagnosed as having it, and the first reaction is "why me?" and anger and all that stuff. But then you have to pull yourself up by the bootstraps and say, "I ain't dead yet." That's what I think the people in the industry ought to be doing.

VISION FOR THE FUTURE

Jack Sandner
Past Chairman
Chicago Mercantile Exchange
President and Chief Executive Officer
RB&H Financial Services

Following 13 years as chairman of the board of the Chicago Mercantile Exchange (CME), the longest serving exchange chairman in the history of the futures industry, Jack Sandner was appointed Special Policy Advisor to the CME board in January 1998.

Sandner joined the CME in 1971 and has served continuously on its board of directors since 1977, having been elected to his eleventh consecutive term to the CME board in January 1997. He has served on and chaired scores of exchange and industry committees. Under his leadership, the CME developed Eurodollar futures, the most actively traded derivatives product in the world; stock index futures and options, for which the CME is the dominant world trading center; and Globex, the international electronic system launched in 1992.

Sandner has testified frequently before Congress on the value and efficiency of futures risk management products and financial services regulation, and he has participated in key economic and financial services meetings, commissions, and committees in the United States and abroad.

Since 1978, Sandner has been president and chief executive officer of RB&H Financial Services L.P., a futures commission merchant and clearing member firm of the CME with 78 offices serving futures clients.

In addition to his many futures industry responsibilities and honors, he has received a number of other awards including the Horatio Alger Award in 1998; American Ireland Fund Man of the Year Award in 1997; Brazilian-American Person of the Year in 1996; Point of Light Award for Excellence in Corporate Community Service for Amicus, a volunteer organization he founded at the CME; and Man of the Year by the Juvenile Diabetes Foundation in 1993.

A member of the Illinois Bar since 1968, Sandner also serves as a trustee of the University of Notre Dame, Roosevelt University, and Rush-Presbyterian-St. Luke's Medical Center and is on the boards of a number of other civic and industry organizations.

As chairman of the Chicago Mercantile Exchange for many years, you have achieved a reputation for your visionary ideas, for helping to shape the exchange and the futures industry, and for your role as a spokesman for futures trading as a whole. Many things have happened quickly in 1998 that bear out your foresight. Let's start with an open-ended question to get a little perspective first. What is your vision today for the exchange and the futures industry and how are they shaping up?

Sandner: You've used the right word in "shape." Basically, the world is marching at lightning speed toward electronic trading. I can give you a pretty sound argument why open outcry is still the better venue of trading today.

An electronic trading system can match open outcry's liquidity and bid/offer spread in a market that has low volatility and also has a very homogeneous constituency—for example, four banks trading with each other in a market that is "5 bid/6 offer" all day. They don't need order fillers and locals generating the engine of liquidity and bids and offers. You could do what they need with a black box.

The other side of that coin is a market that has cycles of volatility and a complex, heterogeneous constituency—retail customers, big institutions, portfolio managers, all sorts of customers—coming together in a pit, trading a product that is influenced by an employment report, interest rates, etc. No electronic system at this time can match, in my opinion, what open outcry will do for you.

That being said, there is also a cost that seems to be very apparent in open outcry in terms of a charge to fill an order and a local making a market and needing to earn money to do it. That money comes out of the system. If seat prices were at $900,000 like they used to be here, it means the locals and the order fillers are making a lot of money. That comes out of the pockets of the ultimate treasury of what that product produces in terms of money for people.

If you could take that money and put it back into the product where the banks are not paying it to get the orders done, they are better off. But what most don't see is that there is a tremendous expenditure if you don't have the locals in terms of a wide bid/offer spread. They don't really see that it's better to pay the $5 or $10 or whatever to the local and order fillers than it is to lose it in the bid/offer, which might cost them $25, $50, or much more.

Other exchanges and the CME are trying to build an electronic trading system that will match the liquidity provided by open outcry. But that system will have to embrace and capitalize on the mindset and the energy and the capital of the market-maker—de facto, the local in our pit. That will require a front end that is a little different than a pure vanilla matching front end.

Banks and those kind of traders are used to that kind of system, but the mindset of a local trader providing liquidity is a little different—call them attention deficit disorders without the Ritalin. You have to give them a different front end that will get them excited. You really don't want to disenfranchise 2000 well-capitalized entrepreneurs; no business entity would want to do that.

So far, no system has been able to embrace that mindset. We can argue about DTB (Deutsche Terminbörse) or other systems or we can argue that we have not had an open-outcry system in any other part of the world that even comes close to matching the well-capitalized entrepreneurs who are in Chicago. Most of the traders at the foreign exchanges are employees of firms and have a different spirit and a different depth of liquidity compared to the two exchanges in Chicago.

Although it is important to understand all that, the real question is, Does it drive the ultimate decision? My answer is No. What my analysis would conclude is that, although open outcry is better, there eventually will be an electronic trading system that can match open outcry.

But, as an exchange, you cannot wait for that to happen because, once you become aware there is that system, someone else will have already begun to take your product. By the time you make the switchover to this system, it might be too late. So you have to be the captain and the shaper of your own destiny. Bite the bullet and understand there will be this system some day, and you might as well be involved in developing and shaping it.

There is another reason to make the change to electronic trading before the perfect system is available. When momentum starts in a direction, your case for open outcry cannot stop the tidal wave of momentum. If firms, portfolio managers, and all the others are talking about match-ups and electronic trading because they keep hearing about it, they start to conclude, it must be good; we want to use it. It's marketing, the hidden persuader. They will never make the fine, subtle, empirical distinction between the cost of open outcry versus electronic trading in the form of bid/offer spreads in a volatile market.

All the open-outcry arguments won't make any difference. To stand against the tidal wave would be absolute malfeasance for an exchange leader to do that to your membership. No matter what the membership is screaming at you, you have to lead them and show them there are several reasons why we have to go to that format.

How do you move to that format?

Sandner: This is the critical question. The challenge is to create a business plan that is inclusive for the local and order filler as well—a plan that raises the tide for everyone and creates value. I will use the example of Microsoft, which did something different from anyone else. It took what I call the "business web" concept and developed a technological web that became so standardized and so predominant that anyone developing any software is writing to the standard that Microsoft has because it would be business lunacy to try to circumvent that. If you want to sell software, you have to develop for Microsoft. So Microsoft becomes the business web, and the spokes of the wheel are everyone else. I would call a business web like that a "shaper."

If you look at that as an example in our business, where everybody seems to be moving toward electronic trading, you can get out in front and be a shaper, or you can be what I would call a "shapee" or an "adapter." You can be a senior partner or a junior partner, a licensor or licensee. A shaper with a plan says, "Let's develop the software quickly—the matching engine and the front end—or buy it. Let's develop a network and common message switch."

The Merc went to NSC in France for our Globex$_2$ system. The front-end screens are provided by GL Consultants, which is owned by the SBF Group, the bourse in Paris, Reuters, and private shareholders. The matching engine is the NSC platform, an excellent French matching system developed by the French bourse. That is the new electronic platform for matching trades, and we started with the GL front end.

The CME will be a part owner, but the key thing is control. You don't necessarily have to have majority ownership if you have control. We can do what we want with this system. We are a licensor, not a licensee. If we want to license it to the New York Mercantile Exchange, we can. You have to have the ability to allow whoever is out there—Bloomberg, Reuters, even small companies—to write an API that would allow people on their front ends to come right into the Globex (CME) system.

So you become a shaper. If you do these kinds of things, you have (1) control of your destiny and (2) no limitation on what product you can trade or the currency in which it is denominated. I say this because I am going to get to a very important point—I know you are just sitting there waiting to ask me about the Chicago Board of Trade (CBOT).

Right now, we have a border around our exchanges. Anyone who wants to buy a membership to be a market-maker and come to the floor has to live in Chicago and has to come to 141 West Jackson (CBOT) or 30 South Wacker (CME). Technology has taken that border away and made geography irrelevant. With technology, your "floor" can be in your home, it can be in Santa Barbara, it can be at a club, it can be in Tokyo. Now you can billboard your product to the world on your screens and your network, which are critical to your distribution.

If an exchange does not take advantage of that, it is going the wrong way on a one-way street. The web I suggest we create would have access to trade all products in the world, whatever they might be or whatever new products financial engineering develop. If you are a shapee and go to someone else's web, you do not control the software, and they limit what you can trade. For example, if they say you can only trade dollar-denominated products, you have now limited yourself. What you have done is look out over the vast global landscape that electronic trading has opened up with its prospects for a worldwide audience with limitless opportunities and drawn your own border around the United States.

That will happen to you if you make alliances with other electronic platforms that do that to you—they own it and they have their own interest in trading products. What you have to do is either develop your own matching system and allow other front ends to write into your system or you have to buy it or you have to joint venture it without any limitations on what you can trade. Then you have the shaper web, the business web, the electronic platform web. That's the strategic plan I would suggest to an exchange, certainly the CME.

Okay, now about that CBOT deal. . . .

Sandner: The CBOT signed a deal with Eurex, the European exchange, in August 1998. In my opinion, it is a ridiculous deal for their membership to buy into. The CBOT is not going to own the system and is a licensee, basically, of the German system called Eurex—no ownership, no real control. And it can only trade dollar-denominated products. So the members have drawn a border around their own growth.

What cyberspace is supposed to do is change that equation so your growth is unlimited and you can access the 3½ billion new entrepreneurs in the world spawned by the fall of communism. It is going to take 10 years for that to develop, but they are going to be there. If you have the CBOT deal, you can't trade the products they are going to want; they are going to be reserved for other people who Eurex chooses.

And how many new products are going to come out in the United States? Is the dollar going to be the center of the universe forever if the Euro takes off? Who knows? Is the T-bond going to be the vehicle of choice for financing the U.S. government or is there going to be a five-year note? If the budget is balanced, there may not be enough debt to do massive bond offerings. Who knows? But you don't want to limit yourself.

I would argue the CBOT decision is a fatal decision for the growth of that institution. As you can see, I have a completely different philosophy to create our own business web, our electronic platform web for the world to write into. We are going to continue forging ahead with NSC and GL with an ownership interest and certainly control. We are talking to everyone and will probably build other alliances, but those will not limit us in our growth. They will nurture it.

We are here to stay in terms of this industry. That doesn't mean the Merc is here to stay or the Board of Trade is here to stay. The Board of Trade has a new building—I got criticized for calling it the Taj Mahal although I didn't really say it that way— but I am loathe to build things that require a lot of bricks and mortar when we are going into a technological era. It's like the move to long-distance learning. Who is building a new college with all sorts of bricks and mortar? You can't find them. Some schools may die with their bricks and mortar because people are going to get their degrees through distance learning. So you don't build bricks and mortar in the face of technology delivering and imparting information.

The CBOT started electronic trading through Project A in late September 1998 right next to, and at the same time as, open-outcry bonds are trading. So it is already challenging the bricks and mortar. That will be a failed proposition for two reasons: (1) The system they are using for institutions in Project A only does 1.8 transactions per second; that makes it a poor test of electronic trading versus open outcry. (2) They are attacking their own pit; it's nuts to do that to yourself, in my opinion.

Another key change that could be part of a strategic plan involves exchange ownership. How will the CME deal with this issue?

Sandner: As the exchange moves forward, it should no longer be a privately owned institution. You should separate equity from membership. Give people paper stock in the enterprise for their memberships. Then you become a much more marketable institution for, say, acquisitions or buying technology. Plus you would be able to change the governing structure so it is not overdemocratized with 88 committees, which make it difficult to move forward. If you are really going to be successful in this era of transition, you have to be able to move quickly. When you have an overdemocratized institution, you are going to get every opinion in the world, and you just can't move ahead. You have to convert the organization to a lean machine that can make decisions very quickly. You also must build in incentives for performance. With a public institution, you can address these issues.

How would this affect the proposals that the Chicago futures exchanges merge?

Sandner: These exchanges shouldn't be insular any more. I have been a proponent for merger for a number of years. If you go back a number of years, people like Leo Melamed said this is the musings of our chairman. Recently, you had a petition with 1400 signatures asking us to merge, and you had a CBOT board that voted to explore a merger with the CME. So now it is not just the musings of the chairman. It is the musings of thousands of people in the industry.

The CBOT signed a deal with Eurex and, to me, that limits their growth. We couldn't be part of that. We could be part of the Eurex system and the CBOT and even merge if they would change that deal and we could come up with a structure that doesn't limit our growth. But we have to be part of being a shaper and not a shapee. We have to be a senior partner and not a junior partner.

Your past ideas about the industry were ahead of their time. Indeed, in August 1998 the Chicago Tribune referred to you as "Sandner, the prophet." Now, looking ahead, what does the exchange of the future have to be?

Sandner: I just saw so clearly that the exchange had to begin to plan for the future and get out of the mindset that we are in the business of open outcry. We are in the business of risk management, asset allocation, and clearing. We are not in the business of open outcry. We also are not in the business of pork belly trading or Eurodollar trading. We are in the business of risk management.

Whatever we can provide to help people manage their risk and allocate and diversify their assets and assure them the integrity of their trade, we must do it. That is the business we are in. If open outcry doesn't serve that purpose as well as the electronic platform, we have to move to the electronic platform. If pork bellies doesn't serve that function any more, we have to move out of pork bellies into something else. That is what it's all about.

Look at the example of Encyclopedia Britannica. It originally had the right vision: It was there to impart information and to educate, and the way it did that was through books. With the advance of technology, along came the CD ROM. But Encyclopedia Britannica resisted, so then its business actually was printing books, not imparting information. The company blew it. When it finally decided it better produce a CD-ROM, it was sold for $995 or 10 times more than the competitors'. The Encyclopedia Britannica hung its hat on printing books when the world was delivering information electronically on CD-ROM for $99. Look what happened. The Encyclopedia Britannica was forced to sell.

That is what the membership has to understand. We are not in the business of open outcry. We are not in the business of trading Eurodollars or pork bellies or S&P contracts. They happen to be the platform and the product that serve our ultimate business: risk management and asset allocation. That is how we have to move.

At the same time we move in that direction, we do have to create value for our members, and they will create value for us as a result.

So that's my philosophy and my thoughts on strategic analysis of how an exchange should be driven into the future if they want to be a player. There will be fewer and fewer exchanges because they will be spokes on the wheel and they will be gobbled up.

How do new trading operations, such as the one set up by Cantor Fitzgerald, affect the existing exchanges?

Sandner: If I had my druthers, I would like to work out something with Cantor. Cantor controls 70 percent of the cash bond business in the world, and it has a network with thousands of screens throughout Europe and the United States. Plus they are beyond the firewall of Goldman Sachs, J.P. Morgan, Morgan Stanley—that pipeline runs into the inner circle of all those firms. They can turn that switch on and 2000 screens turn into 5000 screens.

The whole key to all of this is not so much the software. People can buy that, eventually from Radio Shack, and nobody will care about the software as long as they can do the trade. The key is access, and access comes from distribution. I can have the best software in the world, but if I don't have screens for people to trade on to access my matching engine, I am lost. In mid-1998 Globex had about 500 screens out there. Project A had very few. DTB had maybe 40 screens in the United States and many more in Europe. Cantor Fitzgerald has thousands and thousands of screens out there.

One thing you look for in an alliance is a distribution network. You can have three or four of them—Bloomberg, Reuters, GL—as long as they can write a code to enter your matching system. Cantor could be a potential partner in all of this because it is in the interest rate yield curve so deeply in the cash market that a lot of exciting things can be done with the synergy between the futures and the cash market—plus they bring the network, which is very critical. GL and Eurex both have networks.

That is just one type of alliance; there are all sorts of others that you have to explore. But what you want is a strategic alliance and not just an alliance for the sake of an alliance—and certainly not an alliance that limits your growth. In my terms, an alliance can mean distribution, technology, clearing, and products. It depends on your needs. We have the software; now we need distribution. GL gives us some distribution, but we want more. Whoever blankets the world will capture this part of the financial services industry. There will be more players than one, but there won't be 10 or 15.

You get my idea? If you're a shaper, you've got to have control of your matching software engine and no limit on products; then you have the ability to make alliances that raise the tide for everyone, and you've got to have distribution. You've got to have connectivity to the world with your matching engine. That's the key. That is exactly what Eurex is doing. It is doing what I want to do here. Eurex is creating a web, and the CBOT doesn't see that it is just a spoke in that wheel. They haven't gotten the concept of a business electronic platform web. When you are the web, you are the shaper. Microsoft is the web; everybody writes to Windows. That's what you want to be.

That naturally leads to some other issues such as common clearing. Will that ever happen under the circumstances?

Sandner: Common clearing has been on and off track, but it will probably get off track again. We are supposed to go to referendums as soon as we get done with the niceties of the contract. Common clearing is very important to the industry and, I hope, this time we will get it done. I have been working on this for years, but something always seems to happen to stop it.

Now, the Eurex thing may stop it because Eurex has its own clearing. If we are not part of Eurex—and we are not ever going to be part of Eurex if we are limited on our growth and have this border around us—we could still do common clearing with the CBOT, but they aren't going to want to do it with us because they have obligations to Eurex and wouldn't want us to be privy to their arrangements on cross-margining and other things. Further, there is a very vocal constituency at the CBOT that has written a petition to the board expressing their opposition.

In addition to that, the CBOT membership as a whole probably won't vote it in. They have a lot of members against it, and I've been told it might not even pass their board. It's in their camp. We want to do common clearing; we have for years and we have an agreement to do it. You cannot be insular as an institution any longer in this world of capital demands and competition. The world is merging in every industry—accounting, banks, telecommunications, insurance. . . . They are all merging because, alone, they can't address the global marketplace that is growing exponentially.

The opposition to common clearing also comes from some CME members who believe the initiative that has been proposed gives too much control to the futures commission merchants (FCMs). They question giving up 100 percent ownership of clearing to get a 24 or 25 percent stake in the clearing operation.

Sandner: Their concern is giving up control. The proposal gives FCMs 51 percent ownership but not the control, and members are not making that distinction. Ownership does not necessarily mean control, and in this case, it absolutely does not mean control. I would rather have control and own only 5 percent of this because then I could pay less for expenses. However, the FCMs would only agree to take 51 percent ownership. We have control; we have the votes on the board and the functionary committees. That cannot be changed.

We don't want more ownership; we want less ownership. This is a not-for-profit initiative. It is not supposed to be a profit-making entity. It is supposed to deliver the lowest cost to the customer so the customer trades here. Why do we want to own a nonprofitmaking thing unless we have to? We usually want to own something so we can control it, but if you can come up with platform to control it without owning it, that is what you want. The leverage we had is that the FCMs wanted us to do it so badly they allowed us control.

I think everyone is a little concerned about control of their own destiny these days. As changes take place, what will happen to everybody—the members, floor traders, exchange employees?

Sandner: I don't mean this sarcastically, and I am not the thought police, but if I were them, I would be so excited that I cannot describe it. You have to be totally optimistic. The changes are going to open a whole new world of opportunity, addressing an exponentially growing marketplace, and people should be excited about being a part of it on the ground floor. Those in our business tend to think they are smarter than other people and they can adapt. Some are already adapting, and I tell people: "Stop. Get out of the mindset. Get out of the nine dots. Draw the line outside the nine dots and you'll think of 50 ideas tonight before you go to bed."

This is like technology, which I call creative destruction. Every so many years—three years, five years—whatever you have created is superceded because something better is created. You can't sit on your old technology. There is no indication that the fast-paced change in technology is going to slow down.

The same is true in our industry today. In my opinion the changes could create a whole new Treasury market with cash and futures trading together electronically. All sorts of industries will be created out of this. Yes, there will be some dislocations. Some people will never see their way out of being a local in the pit and won't be able to move to the screen. But for every dislocation, there will be five others who will be able to find opportunity on the screen.

On an individual basis, I can't tell you what will happen, but on a systemic basis throughout the community, people will adapt. It is our challenge to help them adapt and to give them the courage and the optimism and the nurturing to adapt. It is our responsibility to help them along in that process. But there is going to be boundless opportunity out there as a result of all this.

What products or market areas are most vulnerable to change in the next five years? What could disappear? What new contracts might we see?

Sandner: Because of the electronic platform and the Internet and the continued growth in all sorts of industries that will respond with a new entrepreneurial surge over the next decade, your only limit on products is your imagination. The critical thing is you will be able to list these products much more easily on an electronic format and sunshine them, billboard them, parade them to the world in a nanosecond. You have the best marketing format to get to the world, and the world will have easy access to look at your products. Furthermore, through data collection and analysis made easy by technology, you will be able to identify needs in the global arena quicker and more reliably. From there, new products will be born.

The world is developing two things simultaneously in a large way and at lightning speed: (1) It is becoming economically literate like it has never been before and (2) it is becoming technologically literate. With the confluence of those two things, what you have in front of you is a potential trading community that is unlimited. What they have to have is products, clearing, and access.

People who have long been against futures are now coming around to the view that, if futures had not been created, they would have to be invented today because they are so critical and necessary to what is happening in the world. Risk management is going to grow because it is necessary for it to be a part of all the things that people and their companies do.

Getting back to your question, what I see in five years is an enormous marketplace for risk management and asset allocation that is totally global and totally electronic except for agricultural products. There will be two or three key giant "execution palaces"—two or three matching engines, if you will, and two or three clearing entities. That's in five years.

In 10 years I see those matching engines and those institutions coming together and then I see a sellout by all those people who own them because they will not be allowed to own it—like AT&T and the Baby Bells, someone is going to try to break them up. What may happen is a sellout to a world forum entity for billions or trillions of dollars, and it is owned and operated as a utility by the world. That's pretty far out.

Where are the government regulators going to be in all of this?

Sandner: In five years there won't be a Commodity Futures Trading Commission (CFTC). I was criticized for suggesting a complete restructuring of financial regulations a few years ago, but now everybody is talking about it. It's a whole deep subject of its own, but it's called "functional regulation" versus "institutional regulation."

Let me give a concrete example or the words don't have meaning. If you go into a big-city financial district, you see all these huge buildings. They are distinct in terms of the sign they put on the door—Commercial Bank, Investment Bank, Securities Firm, Insurance Company, etc. If you ripped those signs down and pulled the veneer off the wall and looked inside, you couldn't tell the difference in what they are doing. They are all in each other's business. They are all trading risk management instruments, they are all issuing credit cards, they are all selling mutual funds. Yet, they all have a different regulatory platform overseeing and micromanaging what they do. In futures it's the CFTC, in securities it's the Securities and Exchange Commission (SEC), in banks it's about nine of them.

My proposal is to regulate on the basis of function and not on what an institution is called. I have given many speeches and have testified in Congress seven times on this, so it's a matter of record. The CFTC has gotten in its mind that it regulates exchanges, not risk management instruments. That's why it is having trouble regulating the over-the-counter market because this is not trading on an exchange, even though it might be an identical product dressed up a little bit differently. But if it is risk management, it is risk management; if it is capital formation, it is capital formation; if it's deposits, it's deposits. So you have to get out of the mindset of regulating institutions by virtue of what they are called and regulate based on what they are doing, their function.

It is hard for people to grasp that and to turn that philosophy into concrete regulation. But it can be done because the original intent was to regulate a function and that turned into regulating an institution. The legislators should go back to the original purpose and start all over with a clean slate and regulate functions. Why should there be different regulations for risk management because it is in this institution versus that one when it is the same product? It creates unnecessary and expensive regulatory arbitrage.

I believe we are going to move to that concept, and the Federal Reserve Board will probably be the titular head of it. But who knows? Regulation should nurture and facilitate business. Regulators should oversee, not micromanage or become, de facto, the CEO of the business.

With political realities, maybe all you will see in five years is the first step of merging two agencies, the SEC and CFTC. That is probably what is going to happen. It's like other things I have mentioned: Once you see a movement start, it's going to gather momentum. All a new Ag Committee chairman has to say is, "What are we doing with this? Let banking or finance take it," and things could happen very quickly.

I don't know if you can narrow this down, but what single issue or development will affect off-floor traders the most in the next 5 to 10 years?

Sandner: I think they are going to be sitting at a virtual trading platform with a panoply of product line that they have never had access to before, along with access to educational tools and information that enable them to understand the complexities of trading.

If you go back to when options began to trade, they were very complex mathematically and created a new lexicon of terms traders had never heard before—gammas, deltas, straddles, strangles. Traders got educated and took it to another level and then another. People adapted to it and grew into it. And Myron Scholes won a Nobel Prize.

The same thing is going to happen in the future. Traders will have a virtual trading platform that will be accessed universally around the world 24 hours a day, seamlessly and paperless, and the product line will expand exponentially. There will be emerging markets and different global interest rate instruments that have different relationships to each other. The screen trader is going to pick out these arbitrages and dislocations and inefficiencies and take advantage of them.

Of course, as has always been true, not everyone will survive to take advantage of all this, but they will have the opportunity, like never before, with a virtual trading platform to make it ever so easy. Our basic entrepreneurial instinct will be the catalyst as many people—mathematicians, engineers, people who are instinctive—gravitate to this profession and learn to be traders.

We communicate mostly through our larynx. That's how people express themselves today. The younger generation—the

next generation of traders—will communicate through their fingertips on keyboards and screens. Their larynx is their fingers;
their voice boxes are their screens. This generation of traders is
going to grow exponentially because they are going to be given
the voice box in their keyboard that they are very adept at using,
they are going to be given economic information they can analyze and utilize, and they are going to be given the pipelines to
the world to access what is going to be an ever-increasing
amount of product.

The opportunities will be limitless and extraordinary.

CLEARING THE PATH

William R. Shepard
President
Shepard International Inc.

William Shepard is president of Shepard International Inc., a clearing firm he founded in 1984 that later became a nonclearing futures commission merchant associated with Saul Stone & Co. LLC.

A member of the Chicago Mercantile Exchange (CME) International Monetary Market since 1973, Shepard became a member of the CME Division later that year and is also a charter member of the Index and Options Market.

Shepard was elected to his first term on the CME board of directors in 1997. He has been a member of numerous committees at the exchange, serving as chairman of the CUBS/TOPS and Globex Oversight committees and as vice chairman of the Foreign Currency, Dual Trading, Trading Floor Issues, Strategic Planning, Technology Oversight, and GFX Board committees.

One of the overriding themes in all of business in the 1990s has been the advance of technology. How will this trend affect the futures industry and individual traders in the next 5 to 10 years?

Shepard: Technology has been and will be affecting the futures industry in different ways. The advent of computerized trading will bring in many more customers than we have ever seen before in the futures trading arena. Individual traders, nonexchange members, will be sitting on new technology that will enable them to have more control over their trading; exchange members will have extremely sophisticated trading tools at their command, enabling them to better perform their liquidity-enhancing functions as the industry expands.

How do you think order routing and trade execution will change, if at all, as we move into the next century?

Shepard: There will be major changes in order routing and trade execution into the new millenium. Electronic order routing is a must. There is no more efficient way to move orders into a pit-trading environment. For the futures industry to grow, electronic order routing that replaces a myriad of bodies and their corresponding overhead is currently evolving.

As for trade execution, the perfect complement to electronic order routing is electronic trade execution. Electronic trading cards will speed up execution and clearing, thus greasing the skids for giant volume increases that are inevitable.

How will the Year 2000 (Y2K) issue affect the futures industry and traders?

Shepard: Those of us who are mostly involved in the inner workings of the Chicago Mercantile Exchange faced the beginnings of the Year 2000 problems many years ago. Our Eurodollar futures contract trades 10 years forward into the future. At the time we began to list the distant years, we faced many of the Y2K obstacles that other industries now find themselves mired in.

One would have to think that other futures exchanges also have been a step ahead due to the nature of the business. Traders should largely remain unaffected and not see any major differences from current trading.

What are the pros and cons of common clearing for the futures industry, brokerage firms, and traders?

Shepard: It is hard to see any pros in common clearing from the trader viewpoint. At the CME, clearing firms currently own less than 25 percent of the memberships; it is probably about the same at the Chicago Board of Trade (CBOT). Common clearing, as it is currently scripted, would increase the ownership stake of these firms to 51 percent. This amounts to a "land grab," a transference of wealth of significant proportions.

Ultimately, it will come down to control. Even if the agreement, as written today, glosses over this issue, the 51 percent stake needed by clearing members tells the whole story. It eventually will allow these clearing firms to bypass trading floors and cross orders in their back offices. It will end the price transparency that the regulated exchanges have brought to the financial industry and promote bucket-shop-style trading. Naturally, this type of order-matching is much more profitable for the individual clearing firms. This is the lesson we have learned from EFP (exchange for physicals) trading in currencies at the CME.

This is a much different view on common clearing than we normally hear. Typically, the argument for common clearing makes it seem so logical with so much economic sense that you wonder why it didn't happen long ago. What are your thoughts on the role of the CBOT and CME if common clearing should come to pass?

Shepard: If the exchange members elect to form a common clearinghouse with 51 percent of the ownership of said clearinghouse to be owned by futures commission merchants (FCMs) and 49 percent by the two Chicago exchanges, the future role of those exchanges will be diminished, if not entirely eliminated.

The FCM community would gain *complete control* over all issues concerning clearing after five years. Imagine if 10 or 12 of our largest FCMs decided to form their own exchange after the five-year protection period runs out. They could easily divert any business that they normally would place at the traditional exchanges to their new exchange, which would then have its transactions conveniently cleared at the common clearinghouse that they control—in other words, bypass the CBOT and CME.

The FCMs already threaten to pull out of the exchanges in committee. They have petitioned the Commodity Futures Trading Commission for the right to execute block trades between professionals on an off-exchange basis. Their basic goal is to form an FCM exchange so they can take the opposite side of their customer trades.

The Chicago exchanges allow for price transparency in its simplest form. Price transparency, by its very nature, cuts into FCM profits. What they really want is to go backward in time and create legalized "bucket shops." They, for the most part, are inefficient operators and poor marketers. They want to cover up for their inadequacy by bucketing trades.

You mentioned the possibility of an FCM exchange competing with the traditional exchanges. Don't we now have the same type of thing developing in the form of Cantor Fitzgerald setting up its own "exchange" to trade U.S. Treasury futures?

Shepard: Absolutely. Cantor Fitzgerald, a large dealer in Treasury securities and an FCM, actually went the extra step and arranged an agreement with a futures exchange in New York to compete in an electronic venue with the CBOT T-bond futures.

If the Cantor Fitzgerald effort is successful, what do you see happening to the two Chicago exchanges?

Shepard: There is clearly a dichotomy as to what will happen to the exchanges should Cantor Fitzgerald be successful. Pertaining to the CBOT, the volume there could drop drastically to where it would have to list T-bond futures on its proprietary electronic trading system, Project A. This could have dire consequences because the CBOT has an onerous debt and contingent liability situation.

As for the CME, we have currently entered into an agreement with Cantor Fitzgerald and other Treasury dealers to provide our floor members markets that they could spread against our Eurodollar complex. A Cantor Fitzgerald success in T-bonds might be a catalyst for the CME to list the first two months of Eurodollars and serials on Globex. In my opinion, this would fend off all competing electronic trading systems from getting a toehold in Eurodollar futures. It would create the much-needed space that would allow the overcrowded Eurodollar back months to grow and potentially make the overall complex stronger.

Therefore, Cantor Fitzgerald could be a nemesis to the CBOT and an ally of the CME at the same time. It would be an ally for price transparency and would help stop the FCM community that seems hell-bent on bucketing the trades of their own customers.

It seems obvious, then, that you do not favor the proposal for a two-tier futures market that would have different sets of regulations for institutional/commercial traders and retail traders.

Shepard: A two-tier trading system replete with two sets of regulations will only exacerbate the desire of clearinghouses to promote bucket-shop-style trading. The two-tier system is nothing more than a divide-and-conquer strategy. The large New York firms have always hated the fact that the traders in Chicago wrestled back-room dealing out of their control with the price transparency of exchange trading. This is their all-out fight to get it back.

Should they succeed, the industry and consumers will suffer because competition in pricing will be diminished, maybe eliminated. The fact that our regulators are even considering allowing two sets of regulations shows their lack of understanding of the industry, competition, and greed.

Futures exchanges have always been quite protective of their data. Are you suggesting access to data would be restricted even more in a two-tier environment?

Shepard: Wider dissemination of data only serves to benefit the industry by prompting volume. Should a two-tier marketplace be created, dissemination of data will tend to dry up. In a back-room, bucket-shop environment that large clearing institutions are trying to craft, it is essential that online price transparency be avoided. Therefore, we will have to see exactly which way the industry moves. Exchanges will move in the direction of making more data available to attract more customers.

With round-the-clock trading, electronic trading, the Internet, satellite delivery, and all the other means to deliver data and information in recent years, what are the technological breakthroughs that traders should look for in the next few years?

Shepard: The electronic revolution in the futures industry will bring traders to the edge of the pit. It will present the trader, via computer, with significantly more data than ever before. Electronic order entry, electronic trading cards, and computerization in general will bring about online clearing and make price/volume data available instantaneously. All this data will be downloaded into traders' computers and become available for customization by the individual trader. Traders will be able to define their own trading day and manipulate data to their advantage.

Online clearing, electronic order entry, and trade execution will all tie together with the Internet, satellites, fiber optics, and other means to bring outside traders to the edge of the pit. Traders, therefore, should be focusing on the analysis of instantaneous data and the creation of their own custom-created futures indexes and derivatives that the technological breakthroughs will allow them to manipulate to their advantage.

What about volume and open interest figures? What keeps them from being available in real time or at least the same day? Are there any breakthroughs in this area that will help traders?

Shepard: The fact that we have not yet moved to online clearing keeps volume and open interest data from being available in real time. Electronic trading cards and order entry, combined with online clearing, will make this information available in the near future. The most significant change in this area, which will work to the benefit of traders, will be the introduction of "volume at price" data instead of just "last price" data. With dissemination of this new data, we set the stage for meteoric volume increases, just what the securities industry experienced when it advanced electronically.

Considering all the things you have mentioned, what do you see as the single most important futures industry issue or development in the next five years?

Shepard: For individual traders, the single most important futures industry issue has to be the possible fragmentation of the marketplace by putting block trading upstairs in the back offices of large institutions. This misguided effort to deregulate part of the marketplace will create, as I mentioned, legal bucket shops and take what is now a very efficient open single system and shut the door. When this door is shut, individuals will be denied complete information they need to make intelligent trading decisions.

THE BATTLE FOR EUROPE

Jack Wigglesworth
Former Chairman
London International Financial Futures Exchange
Chairman
ABN AMRO Chicago Corporation (UK) Ltd.

Jack Wigglesworth, former chairman of the London International Financial Futures Exchange (LIFFE), has been involved with LIFFE since before its inception. He was one of the original members of the working party established in 1980 to assess the feasibility of a financial futures exchange in London. This led to his participation on the steering committee that established LIFFE in 1982. As a member of that committee, he designed the long gilt contract, for many years the exchange's most successful instrument.

An elected member of the board of directors of LIFFE since it was launched in 1982, Wigglesworth has been involved in all policy aspects of LIFFE's rapid evolution. He was chairman of the Contracts Committee when he sanctioned the design of the FTSE (Financial Times/Stock Exchange) 100 Index futures contract, which triggered the creation of the UK's first real-time equity market index. Before becoming chairman of LIFFE, he served three years as deputy chairman and before that was chairman of the Membership and Rules Committee, the exchange's senior committee, for four years.

Wigglesworth began his career in 1963 at Phillips & Drew as the gilts desk economist. He became a member of the London Stock Exchange in 1968 and developed statistical bond market switching techniques and advisory services to clients. In 1971 he joined a team of economists, actuaries, and other institutional bond market experts at W. Greenwell & Co., where he became a partner in 1973. When Midland Bank took over Greenwell in 1986, he became head of sales for the Lloyds Bank primary government bond dealing company.

Wigglesworth later joined Henderson Administration to set up a bonds and derivatives facility as head of International Bond Investment and was business development director at J.P. Morgan Futures Inc. He then became director of marketing at Citifutures Ltd., the exchange-traded futures and options brokerage arm of Citibank that was acquired by ABN AMRO in 1997. He is now chairman of ABN AMRO Chicago Corporation (UK) Ltd.

In addition to his company and exchange duties, Wigglesworth has also been active on industry boards and committees. Since 1987 he has served on the Authorization Committee and Individuals Registration Panel to the Securities and Futures Authority (SFA), the regulatory body for securities market. In that position he has been closely involved in assessing more than 1350 firms and more than 45,000 individuals who had to be authorized under the Financial Services Act to deal with the public in financial securities or derivatives.

As chairman of one of the world's largest financial futures exchanges, you have been heavily involved in the growth of financial products and the transition to electronic trading. How would you describe the current state of exchanges generally and their future in light of proposals for new trading structures?

Wigglesworth: Exchanges have done pretty well in the last 15 or 20 years, but a lot of technological and other changes as a result of competition are leading some to question whether exchanges are necessary in the future. The thing you always come back to, assuming exchanges can keep up with the technology, is that exchanges will always provide advantages in several important areas: (1) having some centralized pool of liquidity available to facilitate trades and (2) having the clearing function, of course, that will guarantee the performance of the contract.

Regulators, as a whole, may face more serious problems looking ahead. The national regulators don't seem to be able to cope with the new global business that this industry has become, with corporations operating in many countries throughout the world. There is just no way regulators can keep up with everything that companies are doing, patrolling the periphery of the Internet, knowing what people are offering—it's a hell of a big job.

So governments may just have to tell their citizens that if they deal with any old Joe Soap on the Internet, they are on their own—sort of caveat emptor. But if they deal with something that says, for example, "Chicago Board Options Exchange" (CBOE) or "LIFFE" or something like that, they will know there is some integrity behind the counterparty they are dealing with. That is a strength the exchanges have.

You mentioned keeping up with technological changes. How do you see technology affecting exchanges and the shape of the futures industry in the years ahead?

Wigglesworth: I see technology being the key to the future of exchanges, either through the clever use of technology, such as CBOE has done, whereby more than 80 percent of its business comes into the open-outcry exchange electronically, or by exchanges converting totally to operating on the Internet or on whatever network they feel they can succeed.

We at LIFFE have taken the view, as usual, that we will let the market decide by offering both floor and electronic trading, using the best systems in each case. The LIFFE electronic trading system will be available on any PC anywhere in the world through any network. If people choose to operate wholly on that, obviously we will close down those contracts still trading on our floor. That gives people a chance to continue to use the floor where the floor continues to be superior, which it may be for some time yet on things like options or strips or spreads or money market instruments where an element of market-making or negotiation is involved. We are just keeping our options open and will offer both trading platforms.

But I do think one thing is certain: There will be fewer exchanges in the next five years, and they will be radically different from what they are today—as will many other financial institutions and, of course, the way ordinary citizens do many of their day-to-day activities. Exchanges will have to take these steps to be in a position for survival.

What do these changes mean for the brokerage business?

Wigglesworth: Well, brokers are in a vulnerable position, clearly, because it's quite possible for exchanges to deal directly with end users if they so choose. We are very much concerned about trying to route direct dealings through members, and brokers certainly would have a chance to survive if they are in that loop.

The big vulnerability is with clients who know what they are doing and just want execution without paying a broker to do it. Even these traders will always need clearing, so the big clearing members will always have a role, I think.

In whatever field you are talking about, there is always room for good quality advisory services, and some firms will fill this niche. Overall, I think there is a great vulnerability among brokers, who have already felt the pinch on their bottom line in the inexorable downward pressure on commission rates. That has caused quite a number of brokers to merge or close down that side of their business already. And I think that sort of pressure continues.

What about the impact of these changes on your institutional traders?

Wigglesworth: I think the professional traders—those at the big international investment banking houses—are simply going to go where they can get their fills done in size immediately. That argues for very cheap execution and guarantees for getting fills in their size. I think there will be more developments in block trading facilities and other facilities that, at the touch of a key or click on a mouse, will guarantee the execution of their order in the fastest, cheapest possible way.

They are already showing signs of going in that direction. So I think this type of trader will deal cheaply and speedily. I think all the offering services will be doing that sort of thing . . . offering electronic facilities to handle trades through PCs to make it easy for them.

How about the Cantor Fitzgerald plan and those sorts of arrangements?

Wigglesworth: Yes, that is a potential threat to exchanges. But one question for these firms is whether the other big players in the market who might be their competitors will play with them. Firms might not go to a Cantor because they compete in other fields. Just because companies such as Cantor have facilities and screens already available to many people doesn't mean they can list things very easily.

When it comes down to making a trade, what is the reason to prefer a Cantor over, say, the Chicago Board of Trade (CBOT) with the massive amount of liquidity the CBOT offers? Again, if the CBOT—or let's say any exchange—can provide a sufficiently convenient user-friendly screen-based system, my guess is they would win out over a Cantor because, by definition, they have a lot more liquidity and a finer marketplace.

What about international exchange links in this electronic era?

Wigglesworth: I think the days of exchange links—in the sense of dealing in the products of another exchange in a different time zone and helping each other do that when one exchange is closed at home—are over, quite frankly. Some successful existing links will probably continue, such as the Chicago Mercantile Exchange link with the Singapore International Monetary Exchange, which is established and may carry on.

But I don't see any future for any further such links like that because, as exchanges such as LIFFE develop their own truly global systems, anyone with even a pocket PC and modem will be able to trade on it. I don't see any need for local exchanges in that time zone to help out and don't see why you would need the link.

Now, the area where there will still be some sort of linking will probably be on systems. I can see the case for a link, in the interests of the users worldwide, when it comes to establishing common trading systems. And, of course, I can see the case for exchanges attempting to cope with various regulatory requirements sharing information via linkages. But the fundamental idea of links, where one exchange lists another exchange's products that they might grow, is dead.

LIFFE and London have long been a major financial and trading center for both the European trading area and the world. With new exchange arrangements and other new competition popping up, what are the prospects for this leadership role continuing?

Wigglesworth: There is no reason to think that LIFFE will lose its position as the dominant European exchange. We are the second leading exchange in the world, as you know, next to the CBOT in the number of contracts traded. We are fortunate to be in London and in having a number of instruments to trade— short-term interest rates, bonds, equity indexes, stocks and agricultural markets, traded options—no other exchange in the world comes close to the breadth of contracts that LIFFE offers.

We reflect the city of London in international terms. We have the largest international membership—in fact, we are only 24 percent British-owned. The other ownership is 25 percent American, 30 percent Continental European, and 7 percent Japanese. So I think we continue to reflect the fact that London is where most of these markets are traded more than anywhere else.

We deal in the products of all of the world's major currencies, and with the development of the new Euro, I think LIFFE will be the dominant center for trading instruments in that currency as well. I think that LIFFE will maintain its position as *the* major European exchange and will probably continue to be in the top handful in the world along with the main Chicago exchanges.

How about the competition from exchanges such as the new Eurex or other European exchanges?

Wigglesworth: The DTB (Deutsche Terminbörse), which merged into the Eurex, made inroads into only one of our contracts, the German bund futures. We will be using a much better globally coordinated system than the one Eurex is using, and I see no reason to think we won't continue to be the dominant exchange compared even to Eurex. Even with all of their aspirations and getting common links on clearing, there is no way they will have the range of products or the systems in place that LIFFE has. And they are not likely to develop anything better than what we already have in the London Clearing House.

How will the shift to the Euro affect traders? What new opportunities does it bring?

Wigglesworth: It's going to have a big impact on institutions all over the world. If everything goes as planned, the Euro should be one of three major global currencies. The population of the countries taking part will be comparable to that of the United States. So this affects a sizable number of people, banks, corporations, etc.

There are arguments that trading in Euro products will multiple very rapidly. The trading currently in all of the money market instruments in the individual currencies involved in the Euro doesn't come anywhere near to Eurodollar trading. So, if the Euro does become like the dollar in the sense of having clout around the world, you can see the case for a massive increase in trading the Euro derivative products. That's where we have tremendous strength at LIFFE because we have over 90 percent of the business in all those European currencies. We are actually already trading the Euro through instruments that grew out of our ECU (European Currency Unit) instruments, which automatically evolve into the Euro on January 1, 1999.

There are massive implications in the equity area as well, of course. Suddenly, all the participants who take part in those markets—the fund managers, pension funds, and so forth who tended to invest in their local country's currency because that is the currency of their liabilities—now will find a whole new world of Euro-denominated equities. This is going to open up an immense new field. And, of course, the Euro equity index funds are going to be experiencing massive changes. LIFFE and the Amsterdam Exchanges are involved in a cooperative venture with the Eurotop Indexes, based on the Euro, and we see a lot of potential there.

And, of course, looking more broadly, there is a new European Central Bank and the uncertainty about its policies and how it will operate. The move to the Euro will have a massive impact on a whole range of institutions, but it can offer a big opportunity to traders and institutions that can adapt to those changes.

Do you see any particular contracts or markets that are especially vulnerable to change in the next five years?

Wigglesworth: I think there is going to be a lot of change in almost all of them because, more and more, over-the-counter (OTC) products are going to compete with exchange products. Some sort of clearing mechanism for all OTC products is going to develop, which is going to threaten exchange contracts. So I think exchanges and their contracts now are generally vulnerable to the clearing of OTC products.

There is probably still going to be room within the major categories of contracts, such as money markets, for different sorts of currency-denominated instruments. There will always be bond products because there will always be differences in perception of credit risk, even within countries or areas where bonds are denominated in the same currency. Among the equity products, I think there will still be local demand for them and their derivatives.

But, in general, I think this has more to do with technological changes through different platforms and media such as OTC-cleared products than it does with wholesale disappearances of major product ranges.

In what areas will the futures and options industry face its biggest challenges in the next five years?

Wigglesworth: I think it comes down to staying efficient in terms of cost-effective delivery of products. There are so many clever ways of trading—the Internet and all that—that the existing institutional providers are going to be under real pressure against all the possible competition. That's the single most interesting challenge for the industry.

The risk of some major collapse in the world—the failure of the European Economic and Monetary Union, a further meltdown in Asia, or the asset price bubble in the United States suddenly bursting, for example—those are the kinds of problems that could easily cause so much chaos that the derivative market becomes such a casino that no one wants to play the game at all. These problems have a low probability of happening, but you can't rule them out.

LIFFE has voted to move away from being a member-owned organization? How will that affect your exchange's future?

Wigglesworth: A member organization, by definition, builds up very different spectrums of interest among the members and, therefore, makes it difficult to make major strategic decisions about watershed sorts of moves, such as trading platforms. We are moving to a simpler, more ordinary structure without member ownership so we can make quicker decisions and overcome the conflicts of a member-owned exchange.

Would that include public ownership?

Wigglesworth: Not in the sense of a nationalized or government-owned body but in terms of investor shareholders, it could easily. The OM Stockholm in Sweden is a case in point. I think there is a general trend toward that arrangement, although, of course, you will always need some involvement of people at the sharp end of the business who know what the issues are.

Are there any prospects for all of the exchanges in London getting together into one exchange?

Wigglesworth: I always have to be careful when I comment on that because these other exchanges are independent, sovereign bodies in their own right. But I can say there are no current moves afoot to merge or anything like that.

The London Metal Exchange is a little different sort of animal in that it deals with the forward delivery of elements that are dug up and traded on every continent in the world. They are not dealing in contracts in the same sense as we or the Chicago exchanges are. The International Petroleum Exchange is similar to us in the design of its products. Some people think it would be good to have all the products traded under one roof. I won't say it won't happen one day, but nothing is going on at the moment in that direction. It is, however, important for London that we all speak with one voice.

Any final thoughts about other developments in London?

Wigglesworth: Well, we are working flat out to try to maintain our position and our efficiency. We don't have any allusions about the competition or the potential from the chief screen-based systems. We obviously intend to have our own just as early as anyone else does. That's the major race that is on. Of course, locally and parochially, we want to be sure we stay at the center of derivatives trade in Europe.

IN SUMMARY: THE FUTURE OF FUTURES

Scott Slutsky
President
Vantage Commodity Corporation

As a floor trader for most of my life and as a member of one of the world's largest open-outcry exchanges, I naturally became very concerned as I heard more and more about the encroachment of electronic trading and its potential threat to my livelihood.

In a business world of megamergers and downsizing, what were the prospects for my industry and my career? Was the occupation I had learned and at which I had become pretty good after more than 20 years in the pits going to be whisked away with a few clicks of a mouse? Could I find a way to capitalize on what I had absorbed about futures trading over the years by adapting to the changes that inevitably seemed to be coming? Is there life after the pits?

Those were a few of my questions as I contemplated my role in an evolving futures industry. To get some answers, I decided to find out what the outlook for the futures industry was in the eyes of its top players—the people who will be determining what steps to take and how to institute and implement the decisions that could make or break the industry in the next few years. Initially, it appeared that changes in the industry might come gradually over the next 5 or 10 years. But, prompted by advances in technology, so many things happened so quickly in 1998 that it appears that the timetable needs to be moved up dramatically, just as change seems to be occurring rapidly in many other industries.

My roots are firmly entrenched in the open-outcry trading floor. My father was a broker in the agricultural and currency pits for 25 years. My brother Gregg, cousin Jordan, and I started on the floor at an early age as price recorders at the Chicago Mercantile Exchange (CME)—in fact, as children our games included making up markets in gum "futures" and trying to "corner" the baseball card "market" for certain players.

After working on the chalkboards recording currency futures prices during summer and holiday vacations from college, I became a member of the CME in June 1978 and began trading gold futures and later all of the major currency futures. In 1982 my father, brother, sister, and I formed International Currency Futures. At one point in the early 1980s I was one of the largest floor brokers in the Swiss franc futures pit. In my younger and wilder days, I recall a time when I had so many orders to buy going into a Christmas holiday break that I overbought 100 contracts and there was no interbank market to lay off the trade. By the time the market reopened after the holiday, I was down $120,000. That provided a lesson in risk management I haven't forgotten.

In 1989 at the age of 31, I became one of the youngest members ever elected to the board of directors of the CME. In 1996, I established Vantage Commodity Corp. as an introducing broker to handle more retail customer business. Vantage Asset Management Inc. also is registered as a commodity trading advisor, and Vantage Learning Center is a new venture to teach trading and help traders make the transition from the trading floor to screen-based trading.

Even with the new company names, however, over the years my day-to-day activities have been tied to the open-outcry market as business has continued pretty much as usual in the currency pits. Now, as conditions are changing, the traditional roles of the past appear to be in jeopardy. As I began to reassess where I am and where I wanted to go, I discovered the questions I had were important not only to a lot of other floor traders but to off-floor traders as well. Whether you are a hedger or speculator, a small individual trader or manager of an institutional account, virtually every trader of any size in any location will be affected by changes in the industry over the next few years, and you should be aware of what is happening so you can adapt to the new conditions.

I do not want to repeat what the industry's top players have said in their chapters. They have the benefit of far more experience and far more wisdom and have commented far more eloquently than I can. Although they naturally include some "party line" comments, every interview in this book offers unique, worthwhile observations and thought-provoking insights that will help you understand what is happening and is likely to happen in the futures and options industry.

So what did I glean from the responses of all these top industry players? Here are a few conclusions:

Electronic trading is coming on a much broader scale.   Of the forecasts I can make, this is probably the surest one. Fortunately, most traders are adept at adapting to fast-changing market situations, and this shift is just another case where they will have to put that skill into practice. Taking a cue from today's jargon, the message is, "Deal with it."

We moved from the chalkboard to the clacker boards to the computer screen at the exchanges, and I am sure someone opposed every move and failed to see it as progress. But technology is making significant and sudden changes possible, and all exchanges are under pressure to do something quickly to improve their technical systems to better serve their members and the customers they serve. Even during the time I was preparing this book attitudes of several exchanges seemed to change from reluctance to expand electronic trading to one of setting up head-to-head tests of open outcry and electronic trading and letting the market decide which one it wanted. Traders will decide with the flash of a hand signal or the click of a keyboard.

Jack Sandner (see Chapter 17) emphasizes a key point that everyone in the futures industry probably knows but frequently forgets: "We are not in the business of open outcry. We are not in the business of pork belly trading. We are in the business of risk management, asset allocation, and clearing." If electronic trading can accomplish those things better, the exchanges and brokerage firms need to shift to electronic trading.

For reasons mentioned by many of the masters of the futures, that trend will accelerate in the years ahead, especially in the handling and processing of orders electronically and particularly in the financial markets. The bonus may be attracting many more participants into futures trading.

Open outcry will survive in some form in the foreseeable future.   The expression "Different strokes for different folks" may apply here because the nature of the markets may see financial products move to an electronic platform and "traditional" commodities remain in an open-outcry setting until a better electronic system comes along. If a commodity has a production, consumption, transportation, or storage component, it is a good candidate to remain an open-outcry market for some time.

The difference in the two types of markets is where the reference price for that market is discovered. For the financial markets—interest rates, stock indexes, currencies—there is one underlying price, no matter where you are. When the U.S. stock market closes for the day, for example, there is one Dow Jones Industrial Average reading. Whether you are in Lincoln or London, this underlying "cash price" is the same. Futures did not establish that price, although traders do establish a price for a future month based on what they anticipate the market might do.

Physical commodities, on the other hand, have hundreds of prices, depending on local supply-demand, shipping costs, etc. The price of soybeans, for example, may be somewhat different in St. Paul than it is in St. Louis or Sao Paulo. For these commodities, one of the most essential functions of the futures market is price discovery. Buyers and sellers in a centralized market determine a price that usually is the base for prices elsewhere in the world.

Whether you are a farmer selling your machinery or a Sotheby's selling valuable artwork, no method can establish a mutual price as quickly as an auction, which brings together the critical mass of those people who are the most likely ones to be interested in buying and selling a particular product. It will be difficult for any screen to capture what an open-outcry auction market can do—although, of course, at the rate technology is advancing, one can't rule that out. But that day appears to be a little further away in the physical commodity markets than it is for the financial markets.

Even in the financial markets, screen trading may be hard pressed to match open outcry on volatile days unless there are significant advances in some electronic trading systems. You only have to look at the experience of someone trying to get through to their discount stock broker or mutual fund on stock market "crash" days. And what happens when the electric power, phones, or satellites go out? (Those problems can mess up open-outcry trading, too, of course.)

Markets are likely to see more of a trader mentality in the future. Whether it's soybeans or IBM, you do not have to worry too much about positioning yourself in a one-direction market. A generation of investors who have learned only buy-and-hold strategies during an extended one-way move in stocks could be more interested in the advantages of trading rather than investing in the future. I am not trying to make any forecast here about the direction of the stock market, but I am suggesting that it might be wise to know about a two- dimensional approach where it is as easy to be short as it is to be long.

Futures and options, particularly in stock indexes, will probably attract more attention from investors but will never match the audience for stocks for a variety of reasons:

- A sales force of several hundred thousand stock market brokers versus a few thousand futures brokers.
- Most of these Series 7 registered stock brokers do not have Series 3 registration to handle futures trading. They can only make money on Series 7 products. What do you think they will push? What do you think they will bad-mouth?
- Traders have to establish separate accounts for stocks and futures—no cross-margining.

- Large brokerage firms do not make it easy to trade options, especially to go short.

Nevertheless, futures and options continue to gain more acceptance in financial circles, and that should increase in the two-way markets of the future.

Exchange ownership is likely to change in at least a few cases.   Exchanges traditionally have been owned only by members and operated by and for the membership. However, even as this book was being prepared, two exchanges, the CME and the London International Financial Futures Exchange, announced they planned to look at new ownership structures, including the possibility of going public.

If an exchange had a dynamite plan for the future and needed money to implement the plan and if it could structure a deal carefully to be fair to both members and the public, public ownership might give exchanges a real spark. Look at what initial public offerings have done for share prices of lots of companies with far less value and far less earnings than one of the exchanges. Members could potentially make their investment in a seat really pay off.

Common clearing is coming.   The timing remains as big a mystery as it has for the last 10 years. When economic reality is greater than political reality, it will happen. Sometimes the Chicago exchanges seem to be just days or weeks away from that goal, but then political personalities become apparent and an agreement looks like it could be years away.

Somebody probably will have to give up something, and that will happen eventually. But, in the meantime, one of the steps that would seem to be the most logical and would make the most economic sense in the futures industry remains up in the air. If this issue can be resolved and if some control factors can be settled, I would not be surprised to see a total merger of the two Chicago exchanges within five years.

Along these lines, a couple of other items might be mentioned: (1) It is likely a number of exchanges around the world will get together to share more information of a regulatory nature related to risk exposure and technology and (2) again, this is not an attempt to make any predictions, but with the fluctuations in the stock and other financial markets, it would not be a surprise to see defaults or other problems in the over-the-counter market, further reaffirming the integrity of exchanges in guaranteeing every trade.

Regulation of the industry will change.   Whether that means merging the Commodity Futures Trading Commission and the Securities and Exchange Commission in the near future, as some predict, I am not so sure. However, because of the global scope of the marketplace today, regulatory bodies around the world will have to find some way to coordinate their efforts better. One always hesitates to say world government or a one-world regulatory agency, but international companies and international traders will need to have more consistency in regulations from country to country in the future. Unfortunately, regulators may be the last to come around to the developments in an electronic trading world.

If there were to be some consolidation in regulation, one benefit could be the ability to trade Microsoft stocks, the OEX, and S&P 500 Index futures in the same account with the same broker. I am not optimistic enough to think regulators are interested in letting that happen.

Education will be critical for the trader of the future.   First, for many traders, that means learning a lot more about computers and how to use them in screen trading in the future. Second, depending on market conditions, an electronic trading system might attract many new stock market investors to futures, and they will need information and education to deal with this new opportunity. For those who want to prepare, there already are potential training grounds in markets such as the E-mini S&P 500. However, traders of the future will have to learn about many new markets and new ways to trade them if they want to tap more of the opportunities that will be presented to them.

Because education and information will be so important, one thing I envision is virtual trading centers or trading rooms at different locations around the world—sort of a mini trading floor where traders can exchange news and ideas but with all the trading done on screens hooked into any exchange in the world and the brokerage firm of the trader's choice. Traders might pay a membership fee to have access to this room, but in addition to the human interactivity that may be important for many people, they would have all the quotes, news services, and analytical tools available to them. They could learn and earn at the same time.

Futures and options trading will be interesting and challenging in the next five years, just as it has always been.   That is another prediction I feel safe in making. The next few years will be a major test for exchanges, brokerage firms, and everyone involved in the futures and options industry. Many things will change, but the futures and options markets are not going to go away, and the opportunities in new markets will continue to expand. Only those who take action to shape their own destiny will survive.

After reading these views from the "masters of the futures," I hope you have renewed optimism about the futures and options industry and confidence to pursue new goals and opportunities that will open up with the changes the industry is undertaking. I know I am looking forward with anticipation to what lies ahead.

ACRONYMS IN THIS BOOK

The futures industry, like many industries, is filled with jargon and its own set of acronyms, abbreviations, contract symbols, etc. Everyone assumes you know what they mean, but in an industry where you now need to specify the city when you say "Board of Trade," not to mention "The Merc," it may not be so easy to recall what or who is behind all the letter combinations. Most are explained as you go through the text, but just in case, here is a quick reference list.

AMEX American Stock Exchange in New York
BM&F Bolsa de Mercadorias & Futures in Sao Paulo
CBOE Chicago Board Options Exchange
CBOT Chicago Board of Trade
CFTC Commodity Futures Trading Commission, U.S. government agency regulating futures
CME Chicago Mercantile Exchange
COMEX Commodity Exchange Inc. division of NYMEX
CPO Commodity Pool Operator
CSCE Coffee, Sugar & Cocoa Exchange division of NYBOT
CTA Commodity Trading Advisor
DJIA Dow Jones Industrial Average
DTB Deutsche Terminbörse in Frankfurt
ECU European Economic and Currency Unit
EMU European Economic and Monetary Union
FCM Futures Commission Merchant, a brokerage firm
FIA Futures Industry Association
FINEX Financial Exchange division of NYBOT
FX Foreign Exchange
HKFE Hong Kong Futures Exchange
IB Introducing Broker, a brokerage firm that clears through an FCM
IMM International Monetary Market division of the CME
IOM Index and Options Market division of the CME
IPE International Petroleum Exchange in London
LIFFE London International Financial Futures Exchange
LME London Metal Exchange
Matif Marché aTerme International de France in Paris
Nasdaq National Association of Securities Dealers Automated Quotes

NFA   National Futures Association, the U.S. self-regulatory organization
NYBOT   New York Board of Trade
NYCE   New York Cotton Exchange division of NYBOT
NYFE   New York Futures Exchange division of NYBOT
NYMEX   New York Mercantile Exchange
NYSE   New York Stock Exchange
OTC   Over the Counter
PCX   Pacific Exchange
PHLX   Philadelphia Stock Exchange
S&P   Standard & Poor's
SEC   Securities and Exchange Commission
SFE   Sydney Futures Exchange
SIA   Securities Industry Association
SIMEX   Singapore International Monetary Exchange
SOFFEX   Swiss Options and Financial Futures Exchange in Geneva
TIFFE   Tokyo International Financial Futures Exchange
TOPS   CME's Trade Order Processing System

INDEX

INDEX

ABOUT THE AUTHOR

Scott Slutsky is a former member of the Chicago Mercantile Exchange's prestigious Board of Directors, one of the youngest members ever to serve when he was elected in 1989. Slutsky has been a member of the Merc for 21 years, and owns and operates Vantage Commodity Corporation and Vantage Learning Center. He is a popular speaker at conferences and seminars around the country. Mr. Slutsky can be reached at slew1@aol.com, or visit his Web site at vantagecorp.com.